NAVIGATING ROUGH S.E.A.S.
SOUL ERODING ASSIMILATION-FORCING SYSTEMS

A PLAYBOOK FOR NAVIGATING WORKPLACE TRAUMA AND RECLAIMING POWER, WELLNESS, AND JOY

DR. TONICIA FREEMAN-FOSTER

Copyright © 2024 Dr. Tonicia Freeman-Foster

All rights reserved. No part of this publication may be reproduced, distributed, or transmitted in any form or by any means, including photocopying, recording, or other electronic or mechanical methods, without the prior written permission of the publisher, except in the case of brief quotations embodied in critical reviews and certain other non-commercial uses permitted by copyright law. For permission requests, write to the publisher.

ISBN: 979-8-9898669-1-5 (Paperback)
ISBN: 979-8-9898669-0-8 (Hardback)
ISBN: 979-8-9898669-2-2 (eBook)

Book design by Dara Publishing.
Printed in the United States of America.

Disclaimer: The publisher and the authors do not make any guarantee or other promise as to any results that may be obtained from using the content of this book. This publication is meant to be a source of valuable information for the reader, not a substitute for direct expert assistance. If such a level of assistance is required, the services of a competent professional should be utilized.

DEDICATION

This book is dedicated to Black women who are one of the only (if not the only) Black women leaders in their organization. Those fighting for change and struggling to be seen, heard, believed, valued, and celebrated within their organizations.

Queen, I see you standing tall on the shoulders of your ancestors and other trailblazers. I hear, believe, value, and celebrate YOU! I salute YOU! You are bold, beautiful, courageous, and often intentionally misunderstood. You are doing great work. You are positively impacting the lives of others and creating ripple effects that will cultivate generational change and impact the trajectory of the world for the better. This is why you are faced with so many barriers and challenges. I know this is exhausting and overwhelming on many occasions. Just know that your tears, stress, hurt, and pain are not in vain.

Please don't give up on your purpose and why you were created by conflating your purpose with a platform. Your job is one of thousands of platforms through which you share your gifts, experiences, expertise, and talents with others. Your purpose is your reason for being, the difference you were created to make in the world.

Know that you deserve better. Know that you deserve to thrive physically, emotionally, and financially. Give yourself grace and permission to take what you need: time, breaks, and breaths. Why? Because you deserve it, and it's critical for your well-being. Don't worry, the work will not stop. This is a movement and not a moment. There's an entire sisterhood and brotherhood that will ensure the music keeps playing while you take time to care for yourself and replenish your well.

Don't give up! Finish it! (*In my Mortal Kombat voice)

Dr. Tonicia Freeman-Foster

GOOD TROUBLE

Do not get lost in a sea of despair. Be hopeful, be optimistic. Our struggle is not the struggle of a day, a week, a month, or a year; it is the struggle of a lifetime. Never, ever be afraid to make some noise and get in good trouble, necessary trouble.

John Lewis (1940-2020),
Former Representative & Civil Rights Leader

CONTENTS

INTRODUCTION 9

Struggling At Sea

01. The New Queen on the Block 19
    At First Glance 20
    Fix-It Mode 24
    Defining Rough S.E.A.S. 28
    Prevalence Report 32

02. The Virus that Keeps on Virusing 37
    Confronting the Invisible Monster 38
    It Is Not a Figment of Your Imagination 44
    Games People Play 48
    Cycles of Abuse 54
    Why Stay? Why Don't People Leave? 60

03. There's No Safety in Playing It Safe 67
    Disrupting Workplace Conformity 68
    The Unbothered Box 72
    My Powerful Lesson 76

04. The Great Divide and Conquer 81
    The New Shiny Chocolate Baby 82
    The Black Confidant 86
    The Black Seat at the Table 90

05. Getting Relationships Right 95
    Skin Folk and Kinfolk 96
    Everyone Can't Go Everywhere In Every Season 100

06. Life Jackets 105
07. The Seven Waves of Rough S.E.A.S. Navigation Tool ™. . 111

A Navigator's Mindset

08. Get Your Mind Right. 123
    Assess Your Bag. 124
    Unpack Your Bag 128
    Don't Dilute Your Sweet Tea. 132
    Return Check to Sender 136

09. Open Your Eyes 141
    Forecasting Rain 142
    Promised Change 146
    Check Receipts 150

10. Boundaries 153
    Work Friends. 154
    Know Their Story 158
    Grace and Accountability 164

11. Self-Preservation & Reclamation. 167
    Forgiveness Is Freedom. 168
    Reclaim Your Joy 174
    Reclaim Your Wellness 178
    Reclaim Your Power. 182
    Find Your Community 186
    What About Your Friends 190

12. The Intersection of What Next?. 195
    What's In It For Me. 196
    Preparing for the Pivot 200
    Enter With an Exit Plan 204
    Plan to Stay or Plan to Leave. 210
    Floaties 214

CONSIDERATIONS 217
   Tips for Black Women Leaders 218
   Tips for Career Seekers 221
   Tips for Allies in Leadership 228

RESOURCES 233

ABOUT THE AUTHOR 235

ABOUT LEIDOSWEL™. 238

ACKNOWLEDGEMENTS 240

ENDNOTES 244

INTRODUCTION

For generations, as Black women, many of us have been socialized by our loved ones, religious institutions, media, and culture to be seen and not heard. We are taught to be grateful for our checks and benefits. To just keep our heads down, get the work done, and go home. And to do what we need to do to keep the peace at work. The question is, whose peace are we striving to keep, and at whose expense?

We tell ourselves that we will be okay if we follow the scripts handed to us, directly and subliminally, by our employer. Will we really be okay? A significant number of our active hours and nearly a quarter of our lifetime is spent at work—that's 90,000 hours on average. There is no magic wand solution for continually navigating a toxic work environment for that amount of time and being okay. It's the equivalent of repeatedly being bitten by ants, stung by bees, or gut-punched (in some workplaces). You would not be okay or well, even if you figured out a way to manage. No organization could ever adequately compensate you for this, and there is no paycheck or benefit worth it.

We have created and maintained the notion of being okay in an abusive workplace as a protective response. Subsequently, we model, teach, and perpetuate this harmful and false narrative to our children, younger loved ones, and fellow colleagues. Truthfully, we are not okay, and being silent has not resulted in us being okay. Nor has it brought us peace or any other benefits of significance in the workplace. It isn't working for us, and it didn't work for our parents, grandparents, great-grandparents, or our other ancestors. We may be making more money than they made and have more material items than they had, but that does not mean we are winning. In many instances, our paychecks, positions, and possessions have become our trophies for enduring workplace abuse.

> IN MANY INSTANCES, OUR PAYCHECKS, POSITIONS, AND POSSESSIONS HAVE BECOME OUR TROPHIES FOR ENDURING WORKPLACE ABUSE.

How do we dismantle this cycle of generational workplace abuse and trauma?

We must lean into our discomfort, speak up, and take action individually and collectively. We cannot afford to be silent, stuck, or complacent and simultaneously expect things to change. Change requires action. My motivation for writing *Navigating Rough S.E.A.S.—Soul Eroding Assimilation-Forcing Systems* is to continue to amplify what is occurring in many workplaces. I will expound on the meaning of Rough S.E.A.S. in the chapter on *Defining Rough S.E.A.S.*

No action equals no change.

My Experience

I've always known that my workplace experiences were not unique to me. However, I had not fully grasped the magnitude of other Black women's experiences in their workplaces until I leaned into my network and communities. I have lost count of the number of times that I've shared my personal experiences, and others reciprocated with their workplace experiences and traumas. As a national coach, trainer, and consultant, I've heard numerous stories from Black and Brown women and men navigating toxic and abusive workspaces and grappling with healing from workplace trauma. Some of their experiences are similar to mine, and others have had horribly unfathomable experiences. Sadly, many of these individuals thought their experiences were unique to them or their workplaces, and many felt alone. My impetus for writing this book is to use my voice to amplify discreet discussions, shine a light on the impact of workplace trauma, and intentionally dismantle its power over our lives, well-being, and joy.

I would be remiss not to acknowledge the fact that many individuals, especially those from racial, cultural, and gender-diverse backgrounds, navigate workplace abuse and trauma daily. I see you. This book is for you, too. At the same time, I have been intentional in centering my voice and my experiences as a Black woman living in the United States, who has navigated predominantly white leadership spaces and workplace cultures for several years.

Although this book centers on Black women, it does not exclude anyone. I am confident there will be many Black men, Brown women and men, and individuals from various racial and gender identities who can relate to some of the perspectives shared in this book. My intentions are not to isolate or create a hierarchy of workplace abuse but to speak to it authentically from my lens and workplace experiences as a Black woman while cultivating space and providing support for others to speak on their experiences through their lenses.

I have two primary goals. My first goal is to inform Black women that they are not alone. This is not a figment of your imagination. Workplace abuse and trauma is real. Rough S.E.A.S. are real. The impact is life and well-being altering, and it can be deadly.

My second goal is to amplify workplace occurrences, hoping that they resonate with the humanity of organizational leaders, administrators, human resources staff, and workplace allies. People passionate about helping and caring for others are being hurt in the process of doing this great work. In the words of my good friend, Ja'net, this is some foolishness! There is no other way to mold it or finesse it. Workplace abuse is ridiculous and unacceptable. It needs to stop immediately. We were created for better, and if we search deep, most of us have the capacity to be and do better. My goal is to illuminate the signs and impacts of workplace abuse and trauma, experiences that are most likely occurring under bosses' authority and leadership, and provide the support that centers the human experience in a way that fosters reconciliation and healing in the workplace.

I would be remiss not to acknowledge the leaders and allies doing amazing things in their roles. These leaders are lifelong learners, self-reflectors, advocates, and action-takers who intentionally prioritize the human experience. They take great care of all of their staff. They cultivate places and spaces where Black women are seen, heard, believed, valued, and thrive. Thank you! In many instances, these leaders are anomalies. I would love to see their mindsets and practices become the norm that transforms all workspaces.

I hope this book and topic garners urgent attention, self-reflection, uncomfortable conversations, healing spaces, reconciliation, positive and immediate actions, and the development of policies and practices necessary to foster positive change. These elements are essential for cultivating a positive workplace experience where ALL team members thrive equitably. Change is possible, and it can start today!

CHANGE IS POSSIBLE,
AND IT CAN START TODAY!

ABOUT THIS BOOK

This book was designed with the busy Black businesswoman in mind. The shorter chapters are designed for reader convenience. I want this book to be more than a one-time read and become a lasting resource of affirmation, support, and encouragement.

This book contains two sections. Section One, *Struggling At Sea*, is dedicated to understanding Rough S.E.A.S. Section One highlights a few of the various ways Rough S.E.A.S. shows up in the workplace and their multidimensional emotional and physical impacts. The purpose of this section is to increase the reader's self-awareness and anchor the reader in reality, leaving no room for doubt that workplace abuse and trauma are not merely a creation of your imagination. This is foundational to the journey of reclaiming one's power, wellness, and joy.

Section Two, *A Navigator's Mindset*, is dedicated to self-care and taking proactive actions to reduce the impact of Rough S.E.A.S. Section Two highlights strategies and actions that will support you in reclaiming and protecting your power, joy, and wellness. The purpose of this section is to engage the reader in self-reflection and anchor the reader in developing the tools, mindset, skillset, and community necessary to become a navigator.

There are two critical supportive tools associated with this book. The first tool comes in the form of the Soul Compass sections throughout the book. These self-awareness reflection questions were designed to prompt the reader's thoughts, feelings, experiences, and actions. The second tool is the *Navigating Rough S.E.A.S.* companion workbook. This complimentary companion workbook was designed as a tool to support the reader in developing their unique and personalized Navigator Action Plan.

The complimentary workbook can be downloaded at www.navigatingroughseasworkbook.com.

LOST AT SEA

She was lost and losing pieces of herself each day. The spaces previously filled with light, laughter, innovation, and curiosity were now filled with frustration and anger. She was justified, but the weight of her anger was becoming too heavy and, as a result, debilitating. She was drowning in Rough S.E.A.S. and didn't even know she was in water.

Enough! Something had to give. She then remembered and reminded herself of who she was, whose she was, and the power she possessed to save herself. The power she possessed to become a navigator who remained steadfast despite the number and magnitude of the waves she endured. It was at this moment that she reclaimed herself! The badass who was created for this exact moment in time.

Dr. Tonicia Freeman-Foster

SECTION

01

STRUGGLING AT SEA

This section of the book is dedicated to understanding Rough S.E.A.S. This section is the life jacket for those in denial or shock, those trying to figure out what's occurring, those overwhelmed and tired, and those struggling to hold on. This section focuses on removing the barriers and limitations that diminish our discernment and ability to take action. We are self-reflecting on our unique journey and the range of emotions that come with realizing our work environment is toxic, oppressive, or abusive.

It's the realization of what the situation is versus what we desire it to be. It's realizing the physical, emotional, spiritual, and social effects we have incurred due to our workplace experiences. It is the reconciliation of knowing that we are in or have returned to a situation that treated us poorly. These emotions and effects can take a tremendous toll on our lives. However, it does not have to be debilitating. We have choices! We can choose to wallow and fold under the pressures of coulda, shoulda, and woulda. Or we can choose to look in the mirror and love on the queen that stands in front of us. Appreciate the fact that she is here and survived, even if she is tattered and tired. Know that she is not alone. Believe that she deserves better. Believe that she has the power to take action and thrive. This is the intersection of breakdown or breakthrough. Which direction will you choose?

CHAPTER 1
THE NEW QUEEN ON THE BLOCK

At First Glance

I thought it was me.

- Bell Biv Devoe

At first, I thought it was me. My attitude was friendly but tough and no-nonsense. I was hyper-guarded, on the lookout, and consistently ready to defend my words and actions. Simultaneously, I was analyzing who I needed to be to survive in the organization. I was frustrated, and I didn't fully understand why. My uncertainty made it easy for them to label me as intimidating, not a team player, stubborn, mean, scary, etc. You know, the straight-up and sometimes sophisticated gaslighting and racelighting terms used to check Black women into behaving and assimilating when we become too haughty.

MY UNCERTAINTY MADE IT EASY FOR
THEM TO LABEL ME AS INTIMIDATING,
NOT A TEAM PLAYER, STUBBORN, MEAN, SCARY, ETC.

This continued for quite some time. I still couldn't figure out what was occurring. I had lots of questions internally. *Why am I slowly losing myself? Why do I feel I am not being the best version of me? And why can't I stop this from happening?* I prayed and asked God to help me to be the best version of my authentic self. The one who is innovative, brilliant, loving, hopeful, passionate, and funny, yet speaks her mind and holds others accountable from a place of love. THE one, THE vessel, that HE meticulously and cheerfully crafted me to be. I was tired of feeling less than that. I wanted ME back, the real ME. Truthfully, I didn't know if I'd ever fully been myself in the workplace before. However, I knew it was a new day, which presented an opportunity to do something new. I knew my Creator; although I hadn't yet embodied my truest self, I imagined all I could be. I desired, deserved, and needed that. I needed that version of myself to show up. I also needed to know what was holding me back so that I could protect myself diligently. I prayed and prayed. At that moment, my universe shifted, and the epiphany occurred!

Although I was in a new place, I realized that "it" was there too. It didn't follow me, nor did I bring it. It was already there. I was used to it being predictably abrasive, blatant, and visible fairly quickly, like a flashing caution light. However, this time, it was adorned in soft and calming colors, which made it much harder to see. Nevertheless, the Rough S.E.A.S.—Soul Eroding Assimilation-Forcing Systems—were here too, lying in wait like a rip tide in a calm ocean, tucked neatly behind smiles, winks, laughs, and sprinkles of orchestrated care and concern.

They were here too, tucked behind the "we make the world a better place" themed mission, vision, beliefs, and values statements.

They were here, too, tucked behind bold words such as anti-racism, belonging, cultural competence, diversity, equity, family, inclusion, justice, and so on. As if someone had mindlessly gone through each letter of the alphabet and selected a word.

They were here, too, tucked behind the mirage of allyship and solidarity. The kind that talks about it but produces few to no receipts of significance, professionally or personally.

They were here, too.

They were here, too.

Ugh!

The difference was this time, I didn't see it with my eyes at first, but I felt it. My body felt it. It had been trying to get my attention through its manifestations of being frustrated, tired, angry, anxious, sad, and unwell. But I was too far in oblivion to comprehend the signals. I was stuck trying to analyze myself. Why wasn't I feeling it? Why wasn't I feeling rosy and cheerful? What was wrong with me? I was navigating Rough S.E.A.S. and was only half-prepared because I had not fully recognized and accepted this. I thought this organization would be different. Instead, I was struggling, trying to make my surroundings match the image and organizational culture in my head—you know, the one that I envisioned based on my interview.

The one cheerfully discussed by the welcome committee as one of the best places to work.

The one described in the employee handbook and funding proposals.

The one celebrated during the staff meetings and annual retreats.

The one displayed on the organization's walls and website.

The one displayed on banners and brochures at conferences and events in the presence of community members, partners, and future funders.

And the list goes on . . .

However, it wasn't aligning for me. I wasn't feeling it. I didn't see anything beyond words and written documents. And believe me, I had searched high and low. On the surface, it appeared that everyone else was good, and it was aligning for them. So I thought maybe it was just me. Maybe I needed new lenses. So, I internalized the idealized version of the company.

Fix-It Mode

I am and always will be a catalyst for change.

- Shirley Chisholm

Turns out it was not a figment of my imagination. As time passed, there were receipts contrary to the outward-facing demonstrations. Knowing what I saw and sensed was real was a slight relief. I then went into "fix-it" mode. I began to think maybe the "machine" was working. But it just needed some realignments to ensure what we, as an organization, were saying was actually what we were doing. I thought to myself maybe the administrators were extremely busy and hadn't had the time to focus on the realignments. Maybe they just needed someone to help them fix it. Perhaps I was that someone! Maybe this was my reason and purpose for working there.

Excited, I was up for the challenge! I love to fix, strategize, develop, interrogate, and improve processes and systems. *This is my jam!* So, I was more than happy to take a look and try to fix it. After a deeper look, I realized the machine needed significant realignments. There were also parts that needed to be repaired, those that were causing harm and needed to be removed, and those that were severely worn and needed to be replaced immediately. Things were more severe than I expected. *No problem, I got this too!*

However, after sharing my findings regarding the "machine," I understood that while its status was a surprise to me, it was not a surprise to the administrators. Not only were they aware of the broken and poorly operating machine, but they had also contributed to it. They were reinforcing its misalignments and degradation through their beliefs, processes, procedures, decisions, silence, and inaction. Additionally, the machine was being oiled daily with racism, microaggressions, anti-Blackness, discrimination, conscious biases, othering, and various forms of silent and overt oppressive behaviors. It was a lot more complex than it appeared on the surface.

It became clear that they had no intention of fixing anything. And worse, the administrators were resistant to allowing anyone else to fix it. To them, it was not a serious issue or an urgent concern. They viewed the machine as imperfect, though producing desirable and comfortable results. Occasionally, they would highlight and pick a minor part to fix. Nothing that changed the functionality of the broken machine, just a little something to whet the palates of those who deeply cared and were watching. The broken machine was causing harm to most people, whether they knew it or accepted it. At the same time, it clearly benefited others temporarily.

IT BECAME CLEAR THAT THEY HAD NO INTENTION OF FIXING ANYTHING. AND WORSE, THE ADMINISTRATORS WERE RESISTANT TO ALLOWING ANYONE ELSE TO FIX IT.

Any attempts to fix the broken machine would be deemed treasonous and a threat and would be met with consequences such as co-opted retaliation, isolation, bullying, and othering. Eventually, continued efforts would lead to termination (involuntary or forced), which was then communicated to staff in a message that was polished and starched firmer than a pair of blue jeans in the 90s and tailored like an overhead announcement in a department store.

Attention staff, _____ (fill in the name) has resigned to pursue a new opportunity. We want to thank them for all of their work. We wish them well in their next adventure!

The worst was the goodbye parties, where team members came together and smiled, laughed, and ate while pretending not to know the actual reason the person would no longer be employed by the organization. Some of the resigning employees enjoyed the celebration. Some would have opted out if they had the opportunity. Some painfully smiled and counted down the time until the party act ended. At the same time, others felt a sense of obligation to participate and play along for a final time because they desired a "good" letter of recommendation.

The cycle would then resume and repeat with the next resignation. There was no regard for digging to the roots of the problems. Instead, a job posting would be sent out to recruit the next dispensable employee, the next rose seed to be planted in poor soil.

Defining Rough S.E.A.S.

You may encounter many defeats, but you must not be defeated. In fact, it may be necessary to encounter the defeats so you can know who you are, what you can rise from, how you can still come out of it.

- Maya Angelou

What are Rough S.E.A.S.? Soul Eroding Assimilation-Forcing Systems are workplace systems, cultures, processes, practices, behaviors, actions, beliefs, and attitudes that create barriers to showing up confidently and consistently as your authentic self. The impact may cause, contribute to, or exacerbate physical and emotional illnesses, language censorship, hairstyle and apparel policing, imposter syndrome, code-switching, loss of self, voice, hope, and much more.

Rough S.E.A.S. exist across all industry sectors, including health, human and social services, education, hospitality, art, tech, business, and finance. Rough S.E.A.S. occur across in-person, virtual, and hybrid workspaces as well as across various roles and positions, from entry-level and direct services to middle managers, senior managers, and C-Suite members. Wherever there are people, there could be Rough S.E.A.S. Rough S.E.A.S. form as a result of human beings' lack of intentional care and focus on how other human beings are experiencing and being treated by the organization.

Let's be clear: there is no such thing as the perfect workplace. Every workplace has its unique and common challenges, barriers, and frustrations. However, there is a difference between a workplace culture that is frustrating and flawed and one that is devaluing, traumatizing, and abusive.

THERE IS A DIFFERENCE BETWEEN A WORKPLACE CULTURE THAT IS FRUSTRATING AND FLAWED AND ONE THAT IS DEVALUING, TRAUMATIZING, AND ABUSIVE.

For the purposes of the book, I would like to establish a foundation for the meanings of the language that will be used to describe Rough Soul Eroding Assimilation-Forcing Systems (S.E.A.S.):

- The soul is one of the deepest parts of our being. It's the place where our hearts, mind, spirit, and body connect. The place where our mind, will, and emotions meet. It is the core of our humanity and being.

- Erosion is the slow and continuous degradation of a thing over time. In terms of humanity, the constant weathering or wearing down that slowly drains the energy and mindset essential for our thriving. If we are not diligent, we are often unaware of the weathering until it causes depletion.

- Assimilation-forcing is being told (directly or indirectly) that you are not good enough as your whole authentic self. This results in being forced to hide, shrink, remove, or reject parts of your humanity, identity, culture, experiences, and values to be accepted or avoid negative consequences. Forced assimilation strips individuals of their freedom to choose. Choices become ultimatums.

- Systems are a collection of policies, practices, and principles that work together to dictate how a particular thing operates and responds. Systems influence beliefs, behaviors, rewards, penalties, consequences, rights, and privileges. Systems ultimately impact the lives and outcomes of individuals, families, and communities. Systems are created, reinforced, and maintained by people. I believe there are no human systems void of human participation and contributions.

The impact of Rough S.E.A.S. is specific to each individual. As human beings, we are constantly experiencing the world through filters informed by our DNA, personal experiences, and the experiences of others. The cumulative effects of these factors can occur simultaneously or intermittently. Just as waves can vary from a small ripple to a tsunami, workplace abuse also varies in intensity and frequency. Workplace harm is harm, no matter its form. There is no hierarchy of Rough S.E.A.S. Two individuals can work in similar roles and have two completely different experiences at the same organization. What is viewed as tolerable workplace pettiness to one person may be triggering to another person. It may be emotionally traumatizing to someone else and emotionally debilitating to another individual. This non-hierarchical approach to workplace abuse aims to prevent minimizing, negating, and devaluing an individual's experiences and instead promotes listening and asking curious questions.

Soul Compass

Have you ever experienced Rough S.E.A.S.? What impact did they have on your life? What actions have you taken to protect yourself and persevere?

Prevalence Report

If we accept and acquiesce in the face of discrimination, we accept the responsibility ourselves and allow those responsible to salve their conscience by believing that they have our acceptance and concurrence. We should, therefore, protest openly everything . . . that smacks of discrimination or slander.

- Mary McLeod Bethune

This is not a fly-by-night, spur-of-the-moment, or one-and-done topic or conversation. The abundance of data related to the experiences of Black women in the workplace supports the widespread presence and pervasive impacts of Rough S.E.A.S. Data serves as a collection of validating information received through surveys, interviews, and focus groups with individuals navigating similar events and circumstances. Data gives words to our feelings and senses. Data removes the notion of being the only one. Below are highlights from recent studies and surveys on workplace trauma, toxic workplaces, and workplace wellness.

2022 U.S. Surgeon General's Framework for Workplace Mental Health and Well-Being Report:

- Highlights the connection between chronic stress, overactivation of the "fight or flight" response, and the increased risk of diabetes, high blood pressure, high cholesterol, heart disease, obesity, cancer, autoimmune diseases, mental health conditions, and substance misuse challenges.

- The framework identifies five essentials for workplace mental health and well-being: protection from harm, connection and community, work-life harmony, mattering at work, and opportunity for growth. These five essentials are centered on worker voice and equity.

Mind Share Partners' 2023 Mental Health at Work Report:

Among those surveyed, 84% of all respondents indicated their workplace conditions had contributed to at least one mental health challenge.

Based on responses received by Black respondents:

- 73% indicated they experienced poor mental health symptoms.

- 35% indicated work negatively impacts their mental health.

- Only 27% felt comfortable talking to their manager about mental health.

- 50% of those who spoke to their manager about their mental health received a supportive response.

Black Women Thriving 2022 Report:

- Less than 53% of Black women report feeling happy at their job, a statistic which holds true across additional factors within this demographic, such as sexual orientation, age, and marital status.

- 42% of Black women (cis and trans) report not being able to bring their authentic selves to work without worrying about repercussions.

- 43% feel like they are a part of a team.

- 78% report that they sometimes, rarely, or never have the ability to go home at the end of the work day with energy in reserve.

Lean In 2021 Women in the Workplace Study:

- Black women experience more microaggressions than other groups of women. They are three to four times as likely as White women to be subjected to disrespectful and "othering" comments and behavior.

- 32% of Black women who've spoken out against bias and discrimination at work report experiencing retaliation.

- 1 in 8 women of color is a "Double Only"—the only woman and the only person of their race in the room. These women are far more likely than other women to experience microaggressions, bias, discrimination, pressure to perform, and burnout.

---

1 IN 8 WOMEN OF COLOR IS A "DOUBLE ONLY"
—THE ONLY WOMAN AND THE ONLY PERSON OF THEIR RACE IN THE ROOM.

Gallup Center On Black Voices 2020 Study:

- When compared to the experiences of their White and Hispanic male and female counterparts and their Black male counterparts, Black women were least likely to feel valued as team members.

- Black women were least likely to feel treated with respect at work.

- Black women were least likely to feel they had the same advancement opportunities as other team members.

- Black women were least likely to feel that their employer would do what was right if they raised concerns about ethics and integrity.

Soul Compass

Does any of this data resonate with you? If so, which point(s) and why?

CHAPTER 2
THE VIRUS THAT KEEPS ON VIRUSING

Confronting the Invisible Monster

You cannot fix what you will not face.

- James Baldwin

Something is happening in workplaces throughout the United States. It's not new, but it's a topic that is being discussed more often and more publicly: workplace abuse and trauma. Many times, as Black women, we either suffer in silence or silos. We discuss our pain with others who are navigating similar experiences. We discuss how it makes us feel and obtain support from one another. We cultivate and participate in the few spaces where we can just be and just breathe. We depart energized and rejuvenated as a result of being seen, heard, valued, and believed. Then, once we return to our workplaces or virtual workspaces, we return to holding our breath as the energy and rejuvenation we previously experienced evaporate incrementally.

Simultaneously, the emotionally unwell, untethered, narcissistic, apathetic, self-reflection-resistant, and power-dominating behaviors exhibited by a select group of organizational leaders and team members remain unchecked as they continue to inflict and exacerbate abuse in the workplace. The individuals perpetuating these behaviors are frequently portrayed as White men only. In actuality, workplace abuse can be and is inflicted by White women, as well as Asian, Hispanic, and Native American people, and individuals from various racial, ethnic, gender, and cultural identities every day. Black men and women contribute to it, too. Yes, even Black women can and do inflict harm on other Black women. It's sad to acknowledge when someone who has experienced or navigated harm nevertheless engineers or participates in harming others in the workplace. However, it's a truth that we must confront to heal and move forward.

Origins

So, where did all of this come from? We were not created to harm one another. However, we are human beings, and human beings do ridiculous things occasionally. Sometimes intentionally, unintentionally, ignorantly, or due to immaturity, fear, or control. These behaviors are often reinforced and rewarded through social, cultural, familial, or workplace norms. The residue and effects of colonization are real. The United States also has very deep roots in using division tactics to exacerbate oppression, racism, discrimination, homophobia, and other "us versus them" hierarchies of harm and death. No one is immune. It touches each of us but impacts our daily lives differently depending on our intersections of power and privileges.

It's as if slavery and colonization transformed themselves into a workplace virus that just won't surrender. A virus that is pervasive and relentless. It's most attracted to individuals with an insatiable appetite for oppression, power, and control. And it eats for breakfast those who are in denial of its existence and those who don't fully believe in the power they possess to make positive change.

The virus's primary hosts are those who desire to use their power to dominate others, those who desire to be "successful" by any means necessary, and those who continue to focus on their intentions instead of their impact. Even if it means stepping on, climbing on the backs of, crushing, or killing others in the process. If we acknowledge this virus, we can proactively confront it and develop guardrails for ourselves. If we don't, we will continuously be caught off guard and ultimately succumb to it. This virus creates a false sense of belonging. It easily co-opts those who feel like they've never fit in, those who feel unaccepted or devalued, and those who've always desired to be in power as a reaction to their past. Sometimes, this virus even comes with its own manufactured version of God—a God who high fives and gives a nod to workplace racism, inequities, and abuse, as well as the resulting harm.

This workplace virus resembles a domestic violence relationship cycle where employees navigate invisible and yet profound cuts and wounds. There is no time to heal because the abuse is constant, unrelenting, repeating. Employees are left to figure out how to contort into inauthentic, palatable pieces of themselves and are forced to assimilate to frequently changing expectations to survive.

Silence conceals the extent of harmful and abusive behaviors. Silence is a force that enables workplace injustices and inequities to persist, strengthening the invisible monster that everyone sees and no one talks about, confronts, or holds accountable. The silence and invisibility enable the harm to continue by creating a false narrative of skepticism or of being the only one to experience harm. Isolation is exacerbated because there is an assumption that other colleagues are doing well. If you speak up, you may appear to be weak, petty, ungrateful, a complainer, or a troublemaker. Distrust is stoked because there is a fear of talking to the wrong person and of what will happen with the information you share.

> **THE SILENCE AND INVISIBILITY ENABLE THE HARM TO CONTINUE BY CREATING A FALSE NARRATIVE OF SKEPTICISM OR OF BEING THE ONLY ONE TO EXPERIENCE HARM.**

Human-centered supervisors, managers, and directors often navigate the brunt of workplace abuse because they are in closer proximity to the leadership and also in closer relationships with team members and others who are being impacted. These leaders know whether or not any real work is being done to cultivate a better workplace culture. Human-centered leaders are often more severely impacted because, in addition to navigating the abuse happening to them, they also feel a sense of responsibility to buffer and protect their team members, clients, and others from the abuse. We often refer to these individuals as wounded healers—individuals navigating their own traumas as they support others with theirs.

Workplace abuse and trauma are observed and felt by staff within the organization first. Over time, they spill into external spaces, with colleagues, funders, clients, board members, and community members noticing. This often results in side conversations and private well-being checks. However, there is apprehension in sharing. The thought of sharing what's occurring with others causes pause and brings up many questions. Who do you tell? What do you tell them? Do they truly care, or are they just curious? Were they sent by someone to serve as an informant? Will they believe you? What will they do? Will it help your situation, or will it make it worse?

Please lean in and hear this: **no one's coming to save you or us**. We must save ourselves and reclaim our power, wellness, and joy!

How can we disrupt this cycle and reclaim our full selves? I believe by first acknowledging the existence of workplace trauma and abuse. Then, by talking about it, creating a plan of action, finding our community, and engaging in proactive, intentional, and deep self-care.

Soul Compass

Are you currently or have you recently experienced workplace abuse? What steps have you taken to reclaim your full self? Who or what provides you support?

It Is Not a Figment of Your Imagination

Truth is powerful, and it prevails.

- Sojourner Truth

There is a popular commercial on television where the actors spray an air freshener in a dirty and smelly room, cover a person's eyes, and bring the person into the room. The air freshener allegedly blocks the odor so the person can only smell the scent of the air freshener and not the smelly room. Unfortunately, the workplace does not operate like this. There's no magic spray to make workplace abuse disappear. Once you see and experience inequities and abuse in the workplace, you cannot unsee them or undo your experience. There's no more business as usual. The subsequent artificial smiles, laughs, and nice gestures are just that until sincere reconciliation and healing occur.

ONCE YOU SEE AND EXPERIENCE INEQUITIES AND ABUSE IN THE WORKPLACE, YOU CANNOT UNSEE THEM OR UNDO YOUR EXPERIENCE.

The challenge is that sometimes it feels like there is an air freshener in the room, making it seem like others are oblivious to the things occurring. Like me, you may be asking: Why don't others see it? Am I alone? What's wrong with me?

There's absolutely NOTHING wrong with YOU! There are some of us whose discernment is extremely sharp because it's our gift, and our survival depends on it. We often notice things first—sometimes months or years before others can see or experience the same things. We often feel or sense something before we can put words to it. Sometimes, we are tough on ourselves because it feels like we are being judgmental or overly critical of others. If you can relate to this, stop beating yourself up. If this describes you, then this is your unique gift. Breathe and give yourself some grace.

This is not a knock on those who don't have this gift. It's only highlighting a difference. If this is your gift, you are not required to use it to warn, inform, and rescue everyone. There were times when my "early intervention" worked and times when it didn't. I became frustrated because I wanted to help people avoid unnecessary harm. Guess what I learned the hard way? The importance of prioritizing myself and keeping it moving. At the end of the day, people will see it when they see it. We have to trust that our Creator will take care of them until they can see it and take the actions necessary to protect and care for themselves.

If this is not your gift, it's okay. There are no bad gifts. It only means that you have been blessed in other ways. Seek community. There is beauty in being in a community with individuals whose gifts differ from yours. It buffers the impact of Rough S.E.A.S.—Soul Eroding Assimilation-Forcing Systems—by providing additional perspectives and coping strategies.

Games People Play

Mind games do not make me believe you are mysterious or interesting. Mind games do make me believe you are a waste of my energy and a waste of my time.

— **Unknown**

Nothing causes pushback and passive-aggressive behavior more than advocating aloud, enforcing a boundary, or saying no. Everything is "good" until you confront the status quo, comfort levels, and accountability. At this intersection, people who previously demonstrated some level of reasonability and groundedness and those who seemed to rock with you have total meltdowns. Once this occurs, fasten your seatbelt and let the games begin! Privilege, oppressive behaviors, reckless power trips, and fragility show up, along with flipped scripts. Advocates become aggressors. Helpers become harmers. Oppressors become saviors. Silence becomes a threat.

Here are a few games I have experienced and observed leaders play as they leverage, mismanage, manipulate, and abuse their power. It's important to identify the games being played so you can be proactive in developing your mindset, strategy, and response. Identifying the games being played enables you to proactively use your power to protect yourself and effectively manage your expectations. It isn't helpful to show up for a football game dressed and ready to play basketball. Football is a high-contact game, and it requires a helmet and pads for maximum protection against the shock from being hit during the game. Can you imagine being hit or tackled without these protective items? We do this to ourselves in the workplace when we are unaware or are in denial. A lack of awareness of when and what games are occurring in the environment around you will place you at a disadvantage.

IT ISN'T HELPFUL TO SHOW UP FOR A FOOTBALL GAME DRESSED AND READY TO PLAY BASKETBALL.

Game 1: The Maze

Something is always about to start, but it never actually starts. Questions are asked, and focus groups or committees may be formed to work on a particular topic, process, or procedure. However, no one knows what occurred with the outlined tasks or their implementation. Conversations on the topic become less and less frequent over time. Some people are led to believe things are occurring as a result of the efforts expended elsewhere within the organization or that implementation will occur soon. There is so much confusion about the details that people become tired and stop seeking them. It's not until weeks or months later that people realize nothing was ever implemented. Common question: *Hey, do you remember (blank)? Whatever happened with that?*

Game 2: The Never-Ending Surprise

The same harmful behaviors continue to occur repeatedly. The problem is brought to the appropriate person each time, and it's a surprise each time it's brought up. Sometimes apologies and amends are made, and then the same thing happens again and again. Here are some examples:

"Wow, Stephanie! I'm so sorry. I didn't know xyz was harmful. I'm going to strive to do better."

"Oh my goodness, Carmen! Thank you for bringing xyz to my attention. I didn't know it would impact people that way. I'll be sure not to do that again."

"Patrick! I'm sorry that hurt you. Thank you for letting me know how harmful xyz was. I appreciate you taking the time to share that with me. Thank you for teaching me that."

And the cycle continues.

Game 3: Who's Seen My Power

Power plays are consistently made in all types of situations. However, when it's time to make an uncomfortable decision, no one knows who or where the power lies to make the final decision. Each person points to another person or a "system" as the resolution—a system that conveniently never seems to have a leader or point of contact. The power becomes like a set of missing car keys. To no avail, people are looking in their desks, under the sofa, in the pockets of previously worn jeans, and in secret purse compartments. Often, the power to make the final decision is never found. No actions are taken, and no resolution is established.

Game 4: Phantom Folk

Decisions are being made based on secret meetings with unknown persons. Sometimes, the meetings did occur. Sometimes, they did not. Sometimes, the people are real. Sometimes, they are not. Sometimes, an individual met with themselves and changed the I to us. Sometimes, two or three people met, and the sentiments of the small group became the sentiments of "everyone" or "the majority." Here are some examples: "We feel you are . . ." "A majority of the staff feel . . ." "Based on what everyone has shared . . ." "People believe . . ." This game prevents individual conversations and instead focuses on a pile-on approach to creating a power imbalance.

Game 5: Faux Allyship

This self-proclaimed ally always verbalizes their support but cannot produce substantial receipts of their actions. Their receipts sometimes demonstrate that they are engaging in harmful and counterproductive behaviors. These individuals engage in behaviors that position themselves to look good, feel good, and gain certain benefits at the expense of others. These individuals are fair-weather allies, and they will choose oppression in exchange for their financial, personal, physical, and emotional gains, perceived or actual.

Game 6: Top That!

Whenever a problem is raised and accountability is sought, the issue is countered with a response that also makes the person who raised the issue culpable. The initial issue is diverted, and magically, the other person becomes the aggressor, initiator, or significant contributor to the problem.

Example:

Thank you for bringing this to my attention. Steve's actions were totally wrong and caused harm. Your response could have been better as well. In the future, you need to work on your facial expressions and use better words to describe your feelings. You may want to check online to see if there is training for that.

Game 7: Throw the Rock and Hide the Hand

This is a saying frequently shared by the elders in my community. This is when someone instigates or causes a problem, and when confronted, they become the victim. They refuse to take responsibility for their actions. Instead, they pitch one-sided and fabricated stories where they minimize their contributions (if they own up to them at all) and maximize the responder's actions. This garners support, attention, pity, and protection from others unaware of the real story. This is also a go-to approach for narcissistic leaders.

Game 8: Shallow Haling

This is when someone exhibits perspectives in extreme contrast or opposite to what other individuals in the workplace are experiencing. This individual sees few to no issues with the organization's culture despite evidence that the culture is harming others. There is a level of delusion and alternate realities. There may also be more profound underlying mental health challenges at work. Whatever the underlying causes, it is extremely important to understand what you are up against. How can you discuss or expect change from someone who doesn't see a problem in the face of evidence? As my mom says, it's like talking to a wall or banging your head against one and trying to get a response.

Soul Compass

Have you ever experienced any of these games? Did you experience other games that are not listed above? How did they impact you? How have you sharpened your awareness tools?

Cycles of Abuse

Deal with yourself as an individual worthy of respect, and make everyone else deal with you the same way.

- Nikki Giovanni

As we discuss Rough S.E.A.S., it is crucial to focus on the fact that this is not some type of mysterious occurrence. These behaviors most often have underlying pathological and racist roots, as discussed by Dr. Carl Bell in his article titled, Racism: A Symptom of the Narcissistic Personality. This is abuse. In reflecting on the behaviors that I have experienced and observed and those that have been shared with me by others, some patterns surfaced. This led me to dig deeper. I reviewed research on the topics of workplace abuse, workplace trauma, domestic violence, and the manifestations of racism in the workplace. With this, I found associated research and models on this topic. I selected two that resonated with me the most to share in this book. The first is the Narcissistic Abuse Cycle by Aimee Daramus, PsyD. Below, I describe the cycle and provide examples of behaviors I have experienced or observed in each stage.

Idealization Stage – The leader makes you feel special through compliments and gifts, listening to you, and giving you a nice salary and benefits. They may seem very protective of you and not want you to socialize with team members and colleagues. In in-person office environments, they may come to your office to visit you and invite you to lunch regularly.

Devaluation Stage – This is the mind game stage. The leader will accuse you of ignoring them, hurting their feelings, talking about them, and other things you did not do. They may engage in passive-aggressive behavior and then gaslight you when you bring it to their attention. This is a form of "throwing the rock and hiding the hand" game.

Repetition Stage – The leader will begin to isolate and other you to make you internalize what is occurring. They may have random meetings with team members with similar roles and "mistakenly" or intentionally not invite you. If you respond with efforts to distance yourself, you will be met with anger and retaliation. If you respond with actions to improve the relationship, your efforts will be met with temporary positive responses and then a return to harmful and hurtful behaviors from the leader. This is a lose-lose situation.

Discard Stage – This is the end or near completion of the relationship. Either the leader or the employee decides they are finished with the relationship. If the leader chooses to, they may cite reasons such as you being untrustworthy, aggressive, or lacking alignment with their goals for the organization. They may even attempt to attack your character as a human being to gain buy-in or approval from others. The relationship may also end if you leave the organization or their department. The leader may or may not adjust their perspectives of the situation upon your departure.

The second model I selected is bullycide (Dignity Together, 2020). It is when the cause of suicide can be attributed to the bullying of an individual at work. Research demonstrates a connection between workplace bullying and suicide. Individuals who are exposed to workplace bullying are one to three times more likely to have suicidal ideations and death by suicide when compared to their peers who have not been exposed to workplace bullying (Magnusson Hanson et al., 2023). Below, I describe the cycle and provide examples of behaviors I have experienced or observed in each phase of the process. The model is rooted in an abuse of power by the abusive leader and manipulation of others to believe the targeted employee is the problem, using the following or similar processes:

1. The abusive leader reprimands the targeted employee for trivial matters. Employees may receive a talking-to, verbal warning, or written reprimand for not cleaning their desks, looking disengaged during a meeting, being too expressive during a meeting, not responding to a last-minute meeting notice, or being a few minutes late returning from lunch or break.

2. The abusive leader convinces others the targeted employee is incompetent. The abusive leader may scrutinize the

target employee's work more harshly. They may magnify minor mistakes by distorting the frequency or severity of the mistake or blatantly lie about the employee's work. This may be casually presented in conversations with fellow employees or external colleagues, creating a pile-on effect enabling others to adopt their stories about the targeted employee.

3. The abusive leader drives the target to report the problem, which worsens the problem. The abusive leader continues to reprimand the targeted employee to the point where the employee feels like there is no way to improve the situation independently, so they seek support from a higher authority or HR. Often, the reprimands are mostly verbal, meaning there is no record of the conversations. This, in turn, makes the targeted employee appear to be hypersensitive, unstable, and not a team player. It also allows the abusive leader to continue with little to no accountability for their actions. Once the abusive leader is reported, they go into overdrive on the written reprimands.

4. The abusive leader's behavior is so outrageous that it is difficult for the targeted employee's friends or family to believe it or provide support. The abusive leader may undermine the targeted employee by meeting with their direct reports without their knowledge, going through their desk or personal artifacts while they are away, denying leave requests without cause, and showing up to meetings they would not normally attend. These behaviors are extremely harmful yet childlike in nature, making it easy for them to be disbelieved and minimized by others.

5. The targeted employee is alone and isolated, which places them at increased vulnerability to suicidal ideations and suicide. At this point, the targeted employee is tired of explaining and trying to convince others about what is happening in their workplace. Simultaneously, they have reached a point where they can no longer carry the weight

of everything on their own. They may be unable to identify a positive or healthy way of navigating the workplace environment and feel they have no other viable options.

Soul Compass

Have you experienced or observed any of these behaviors? What was your response? Would you respond in the same way today or choose a different response?

Why Stay? Why Don't People Leave?

In every crisis, there is a message. Crises are nature's way of forcing change — breaking down old structures, shaking loose negative habits so that something new and better can take their place.

- Susan L. Taylor

According to the American Psychological Association, more than one in five employees have experienced harm to their mental health at work (American Psychological Association, 2023), and based on the research previously shared, Black women are disproportionately impacted. A 2022 report from Black Women Thriving (BWT) highlights that three in five Black women report not feeling emotionally safe at work (Agbanobi & Asmelash, 2023). This is a critical issue that organizational leaders must prioritize if their goal is to create healthy work cultures.

Now, you might be wondering, "Why stay?" "Why don't people just leave?" In the previous chapter, we discussed the cycle of abuse as an illustration of how easy it is to become emotionally trapped in an abusive workplace. There are a multitude of reasons why people stay in toxic work environments. These reasons include but are not limited to their love for clients/patients, customers, and colleagues; salary and benefits; financial obligations and debt; their position is connected to a family legacy of success or being the first; feeling stuck; awaiting the perfect opportunity; waiting for the problem to leave or retire; leaving feels like giving up too easily; or fear of leaving and things not working out well in their next venture.

Reflecting on my workplace experiences, I thought about all the times I should have left but didn't. I began to think about the forces that were keeping me there. There was the impact of the external forces, which by all means were telling me the environment was harmful, no positive changes were coming anytime soon, and that it was in my best interest to leave. Simultaneously, strong internal forces were at work, playing on my beliefs about my reason for being and my purpose in life. I believed that I needed to stay to protect and buffer the harm to my team members. I believed the clients would not be treated with the highest level of respect, value, and dignity they deserved. I believed conversations and actions to ensure equity, inclusion, anti-racism, and justice would fade away in my absence. I believed community-based practices would be devalued and replaced by evidence-based practices that limited or removed the voices of the individuals who were most affected. I believed innovative community collaborations and partnerships would dissipate.

These were all valid reasons and concerns for me to stay. It wasn't until a conversation with a wise mentor who was aware of the situation that my eyes were opened. He said, "You were not placed here to save anyone. You are not Mother Tonicia. The people will be fine. They will figure it out and do what they need to do to care for themselves. The Creator will take care of them." Wow! That released so much weight off my shoulders, giving me the space and mindset that I needed to make a guilt-free decision in my best interest. After all, I had been committed as a leader not to create dependencies but always to prepare my team to advocate for themselves, take positive risks, and care for themselves and one another. Now, it was my turn to take care of myself and bust a move! Ultimately, my mentor's advice turned out to be right. Nearly all of my team members did what they needed to do to care for themselves. For some, this meant leaving the organization; for others, it meant staying and navigating the culture while implementing strong self-care practices.

THE PEOPLE WILL BE FINE. THEY WILL FIGURE IT OUT AND DO WHAT THEY NEED TO DO TO CARE FOR THEMSELVES.

Why do people stay in toxic workplaces? For the same or similar reasons we stay in other toxic relationships. It's easy to ask, "Why don't you just leave?" I've heard it several times and asked this and other questions to myself often while navigating abusive work environments. What was really holding me there? Why was I able to see the harm being done but was still unable to walk away? Based on my experiences, I hypothesize that the actual and perceived benefits must outweigh the actual and perceived costs. The weight necessary to cultivate change is based on the individual and can be categorized as a tipping point. What is a tipping point?

Merriam-Webster Dictionary defines a tipping point as the critical point in a situation, process, or system beyond which a significant and often unstoppable effect or change occurs (Merriam-Webster Dictionary, 2023). In his book, *The Tipping Point: How Little Things Can Make a Big Difference*, Malcolm Gladwell describes a tipping point as that magical moment when an idea, trend, or social behavior crosses a threshold, tips, and spreads like wildfire. I like to think of it through the lens of a kettle, from the point of being filled with water to the point at which the water begins to boil and whistle. Ultimately, a tipping point is the intersection where potential transforms into action.

From the Outside Looking In

Sometimes, people, especially those on the outside, don't fully understand what's going on. So, in turn, they may not fully understand how you are being impacted and why you are contemplating leaving or staying. This is why it is extremely important to be mindful of who you are talking to and their capacity to provide sound support. There are abusive organizations that have been in business for years, have accumulated wealth, pay excellent salaries, and provide great benefits. Many of these organizations are perceived to be a model of success by those who are on the outside looking in. This compounds the decision to leave or stay, as things look glossy on the outside, so leaving seems ridiculous to others. Some people will be perplexed by you even contemplating leaving. Some familiar responses I've heard are, "*Girl, I wish I had a job that paid me that much,*" "*Girl, the benefits they provide are some of the best,*" or "*Girl, is it that bad over there? I can show you bad. It's too bad we can't switch places; I would take working there over working here in a heartbeat.*" These responses are common and to be expected from those who love you, those who are afraid for you to leave, and those who have a mentality of money over everything. Some may believe money is more important than your health, well-being, and joy as if these things can be purchased later or are on a never-ending replacement and replenishment cycle. Sometimes, we are those people, and we are the voice that contributes these thoughts to ourselves through self-talk and doubt in our abilities to succeed outside our current organization.

The truth is that some things can be lost and never fully recovered. Your peace, joy, and health are priceless and should not be taken for granted. I know several people whose health has been severely impacted for various reasons, affecting the quality of their lives and those around them. We only get one life. Life is unlike a video game where you can accumulate lives or drink magic potions to restore parts of yourself that were stolen in previous seasons. There is no job, amount of money, or benefits plan worth losing yourself. You have gifts that make your community and the world a better place. These gifts are unique to you and are the divine difference that you were created to make. If you are not here, the world loses out on what you were supposed to bring.

Imagine a holiday spread of food. There can be 100 amazing choices on the table. However, there is one dish made by a specific individual that you have been anticipating for days. This dish takes the holiday spread over the top for you. This dish is the connector that levels up the other food on your plate. This dish makes your day. Of course, you would still eat in the absence of this dish. However, it would be a different experience. Think about your unique impact through this lens. Imagine your gift being that dish that the people you were created to reach are waiting for. Imagine the impact that you can bring to their lives.

Our gifts are powerful, and we must be protective and intentional about them. It doesn't matter what other people think or believe about the organization you are working at. Do not conflate the platform with your purpose. Your current job is only a platform that employs you for your gifts, but you have a mission and purpose that live within you. It's not on you to convince anyone to believe you or the harm you are experiencing. Center yourself and prioritize your needs. You are the only person who truly knows what it's like to get out of bed and prepare to go to that job each day. You are the only person who truly knows the feelings that arise when you are en route to the office or working remotely and logging on to your computer for work each day. You are the only person who truly knows what spending a day in your shoes, role, and work environment is like. Prioritize YOU!

Soul Compass

What keeps you at your current organization? What do the individuals in your circle believe about your job?

CHAPTER 3
THERE'S NO SAFETY IN PLAYING IT SAFE

Disrupting Workplace Conformity

I don't have any time to stay up all night worrying about what someone who doesn't love me has to say about me.

- Viola Davis

"Pray about it."

"Be still."

"Be quiet."

"Be polite."

"Just agree."

"Don't do it like that."

"You should have said it differently."

"Focus on the good."

"Just do your work and go home."

"Be thankful for the paycheck and benefits."

Do any of these sound familiar? Has someone told you this? Have you said it to someone you supervised or mentored? Have you internalized these statements as your way of being in the workplace?

These sentiments remind me of a photo shoot for a middle school yearbook. "Turn your body to the right, turn your neck slightly, tilt your head, look this way, and smile." While these prompts may help you look amazing in your photos, it's not as cute in the workplace. This kind of micromanaging of your outlook will wear you down over time. Having to constantly change who you are and how you show up to appease others is an indicator of a dysfunctional, oppressive, traumatizing, and growth-resistant work environment, to say the least.

In most cases, you can do nothing to be looked at more favorably except be quiet until you are asked to speak, and then, when you talk, stick to the agreed-upon, comfortable script. Many times, it's not how you phrased a critique, your tone, or your facial expression. It's the fact that you had the audacity to think it and speak it or call it out, period!

As Black women, many of us were raised and have been socialized to strive towards the American dream of that "good government job" with those "good benefits" even when we are being harmed and literally holding on for our lives in the process. We lose sight of the fact that our being, in addition to our gifts, talents, and skills, transcends our workplaces. Not the other way around. The workplace is merely a platform, and our employer is one out of thousands of pathways to fulfill our life's mission and purpose. It is crucial to distinguish between the platform and our purpose. Conflating the two could cause us to become tired and give up on the very thing we were created to be and do. Don't conflate your purpose with the platform. Our purpose is the divine reason that we were created and placed on Earth, while a platform is a place where we facilitate actions that align with our purpose. Our platforms will change throughout our lives. Our purpose will remain the same. However, how we actualize it may vary and evolve as we learn and grow.

DON'T CONFLATE YOUR PURPOSE WITH THE PLATFORM.

When we conflate our purpose and platform, we become distracted from seeing the power of our purpose and begin to laser-focus on the platform and prioritize the goal of holding on to that platform. This increases the probability of us conforming to inauthentic ways of being, believing, and responding. We will attempt to make ourselves small to fit in and garner the approval of others when we were actually created to stand tall, stand out, and be seen as the person who goes against the status quo by speaking truth to power.

From the outside, staying silent in a toxic and abusive workplace may appear like a win. Maybe you're able to fly under the radar and pay off some bills, meet some needs and wants for yourself and your loved ones, and enjoy nice vacations and other material items. Maybe you are feeling a sense of obligation to remain steadfast to a family or personal legacy. Perhaps you are the first person in your family to be in an executive leadership role, become self-sufficient, earn six figures, or purchase a home. These are phenomenal achievements! However, what are the true costs of accomplishing these things in your current workplace environment? What are the benefits? Do the benefits outweigh the costs? What will be the future effects on you internally? What's held inside manifests itself internally.

Being quiet in the face of an abusive and toxic workplace environment is extremely harmful. I have found that saying what I need to say through a lens of love is healthy for me. For me, holding it in is unhealthy, and it has made me physically ill at times. I must also acknowledge that speaking up can be scary and cause discomfort. I have felt uneasy plenty of times before and after speaking up. I believe this feeling comes with pushing against the status quo of oppression and voice suppression and potential consequences. In my mind, I will experience discomfort whether I speak up or stay silent. Absorbing that discomfort serves no one well and harms me the most in the long run. Therefore, I consciously choose as much as possible to navigate the discomfort of saying what I need to communicate rather than holding it in my body.

Soul Compass

What is your purpose? What actions are you taking to ensure workplace conformity does not erode your purpose?

The Unbothered Box

You can pray until you faint, but if you don't get up and try to do something, God is not going to put it in your lap.

- Fannie Lou Hamer

Sometimes, we shrug harmful things off and discount them as minimal. However, there's a thin line between being genuinely unbothered by an experience versus placing an experience in the "unbothered box" as a means of coping. We must be truthful with ourselves. It's okay if others do not see or experience something the same way. This does not negate our feelings, make them wrong, or mean that we are being too sensitive. Your feelings are real and valid.

We cannot fix or heal things we refuse or neglect to acknowledge. Not acknowledging it is comparable to throwing a lit match. Depending on where it lands, there is a potential for it to ignite a larger fire. Depending on the presence or absence of an accelerant, the fire may burn slowly or quickly. Eventually, it will either extinguish on its own, burn slowly, or become uncontainable like wildfire, needing immediate and significant intervention. It's important to remember that harm always creates a burn. Sometimes, the burn is in the form of the fire that we thought was extinguished, but in actuality, it's been lowly burning for years. In my experience, the little fires are the most dangerous. We can see the big fires, tend to them, and begin the healing and restoration processes. However, the low-flame fires that burn for years with very little smoke slowly erode our sense of belonging, confidence, self-esteem, innovation, and joy.

THE LOW-FLAME FIRES THAT BURN FOR YEARS WITH VERY LITTLE SMOKE SLOWLY ERODE OUR SENSE OF BELONGING, CONFIDENCE, SELF-ESTEEM, INNOVATION, AND JOY.

What do low-flame fires look like in the workplace? Many times, the impacts of workplace stress, abuse, and trauma only catch our attention when they become external manifestations. We may experience headaches, lethargy, apathy, digestive challenges, anxiety, minor hair loss, new or exacerbated mental health challenges, and much more. We then tend to the external effects with quick remedies that include prescribed or over-the-counter medications, or we self-medicate through poor habits and routines. For example, we may address hair loss through hair growth pomades and conditioners. We may address lethargy through energy drinks and supplements. We may address the exacerbated mental wellness challenges by increasing our medication dosages. This does not and will not fix the underlying problem. The external effects result from internal manifestations that have accumulated over time. This is how the low-flame fires become wildfires.

We must address both the internal and external effects. Focusing on the external manifestations of workplace abuse and trauma often leads to neglecting the internal manifestations and underlying causes. Consequently, we rarely deeply investigate what is occurring internally, inside our minds and bodies, due to these workplace experiences. How are these experiences impacting our bodies, hormones, equilibrium, and the operations and synergies of our internal systems? What will be the long-term implications? How will the long-term implications impact us and our loved ones? Our minds and bodies are divine creations trying to protect us through unique signals. If the underlying causes are left unaddressed, we increase our chances of addiction, chronic illness, disease, disability, and premature death. I have personally found therapy, individual and group coaching, and being in a community with my support system to greatly benefit my healing and restoration.

Soul Compass

Are you currently experiencing external manifestations due to your workplace? How is this showing up? What actions have you taken?

My Powerful Lesson

We learn our power and who we are at the intersection of fight or fold.

- Dr. Tonicia Freeman-Foster

I felt good. I was walking a few miles each day, losing weight, and eating well. I was looking cute and feeling myself, too. I was bobbing and weaving the stressors at work very well—at least, I thought I was. There was no way anything could be going wrong in my body.

Soon after, I went to my general practitioner for my annual wellness visit. During my visit, the doctor said, "Your labs look great! However, I was listening to your heartbeat, and it sounds like you have a minor heart murmur. I would like to order more intensive testing." I remained calm. I didn't think there was anything to worry about because my other labs had returned with great results. However, just a few months later, I was short of breath. I thought it was due to my pollen reaction from a bouquet of flowers. I checked in with telehealth and was told it was most likely a sinus infection and prescribed medications. I followed up with my doctor and proceeded with the previously ordered tests to assess the perceived minor heart murmur. These tests resulted in additional tests. Ultimately, the testing revealed a left upper anterior mediastinal fluid-filled mass, 13.6 x 9.2 cm in size. It was pressing against my heart, causing a heart murmur-like sound, and also pressing near my lungs, which contributed to my shortness of breath. After a few more referrals and additional tests, it was determined that the fluid-filled sac was cancerous, and the cancer cells were multiplying rapidly. I was later diagnosed with non-Hodgkin's lymphoma.

At the age of 37, I was battling cancer. I had no family history, had never smoked, had no history of illness, and had no prior hospitalizations. Overall, I was in great health on the outside, but internally, my body was telling a completely different story. Even my medical team was (and remains) perplexed by what was occurring in my body based on my age, health, and medical history. My doctor could not determine if this had developed quickly over a few months or slowly over a few years. Nevertheless, I was determined to fight and win.

After six months of chemotherapy and twenty-five rounds of radiation therapy, I was able to heal my body. First and foremost, because of an omnipresent God of miracles, I am still here on this side of the Earth. Second, I am grateful for the abundant love, care, prayers, and support from my close family and friends. Third, I am grateful for a compassionate, praying, and phenomenal medical team. I am here! Alive, blessed, and well. Grateful for an abundant life!

What I learned . . .

Beating cancer was one of the most difficult fights of my life. It was a fight-or-fold moment for me. I am grateful to be blessed with the strength to fight it and the subsequent blessing of a refined awareness of the value of time and life. I believe there is no such thing as a coincidence. If we look for it, I believe there is a lesson to be learned or a silver lining in everything we navigate in our lives. This applies to positive and negative situations. Sometimes, the lesson or silver lining is apparent in the moment. Sometimes, we see it retrospectively months or years down the road. Sometimes, the lesson is: don't do that again. Sometimes, the silver lining is that you made it through with greater wisdom and appreciation for life. Through our stories, we are often blessed with the opportunity to reach over and inspire someone else to keep going. Cancer taught me and continues to teach me some powerful lessons. I will share four of many.

The first lesson is that you don't have to look sick to be sick. If I received a check for every time someone told me, "You don't look sick," I would have a nice chunk of change in my bank account. The human body is a unique and divinely crafted machine! It possesses the power to navigate and recover from so many things: illness, disaster, abuse, trauma, depression, heartache, and much more. It will hold itself together and keep going until it can't any longer and gives way like a tire blowout on an expressway.

YOU DON'T HAVE TO LOOK SICK TO BE SICK.

Second, my cancer journey has made me more aware of the effects of the low-flame fires. I continue to learn the cumulative effects of workplace trauma and harm on our physical, emotional, social, and mental well-being. It doesn't matter if the effects are visible or not; they still impact us. I've committed to myself that I cannot and will not subject myself to working in a toxic and abusive workplace. Does that stop it from occurring? Of course not. Some organizations have perfected covering up what happens behind the scenes. Regardless of how organizations do or do not operate, that is beyond my power. We have a duty and responsibility to prioritize ourselves and our well-being.

The third lesson is the power of forgiveness. When you release others from their bad debt and trespasses, you also release yourself. Forgiving people doesn't mean that you forget. It doesn't mean that you are soft or a doormat. It means you have surrendered the things you have no control over and are moving forward. It means you have freed up space and have increased your mind and body's capacity to embrace new and positive things. It also allows the other person the freedom to grow and evolve instead of being held to the person they were months or years ago. It works both ways: to forgive and to be forgiven. Forgiveness feels good! I will expound on this in the next section, *A Navigator's Mindset*.

Fourth, of course, the researcher in me wanted to know and learn everything I could about my form of cancer. In my research, I found out that in addition to the lymph nodes, the anterior mediastinum houses the thymus. The thymus is located above the heart. It is an organ that is rarely discussed. The thymus is a critical part of our immune system, and it helps us ward off things such as pathogens, tumors, and other diseases. Researchers describe the thymus gland as the seat of the soul. One of my admired mentors from afar, Reverend Dr.

Iyanla Vanzant, describes the thymus as an organ influenced by emotions, especially those related to feeling unsafe and attacked. She often discusses the importance of exercises such as thymus-thumping and positive affirmations to clear stuck energy around negative emotions and to ensure the thymus is working efficiently. This made me think of the number of illnesses and disparities that Black women face as it relates to our heart and immune system and their connection to the unhealthy workplaces that we navigate.

I am thankful for my ongoing doctor's appointments and lab tests. They have enabled me to see how stress and the workplace impact me internally and externally. I can get a pulse on what is occurring in my body through my lab tests. As a result, I continuously strive to prioritize myself by increasing my awareness of things that cause my low flames and big fires and then taking action. It is a work in progress, but it has benefited me greatly. Speaking up and advocating for myself, modeling a way for others to advocate for themselves, and maintaining stronger boundaries have been critical to my balance and wellness. Also, doing my self-work through therapy, continuous learning, self-reflection, forgiving myself and others, exercising, eating healthier, and engaging in a deep and unconditional love of ME has been super beneficial on this journey.

Download the complimentary Navigating Rough S.E.A.S. workbook to learn more about the thymus gland:
http://www.navigatingroughseasworkbook.com.

CHAPTER 4
THE GREAT DIVIDE AND CONQUER

The New Shiny Chocolate Baby

Honey, please don't confuse freedom with arrogance. I use to be a code switcher and it did nothing for anyone. We should be accepted in any room because we are enough! I will never pave a road for others that requires them to give up their freedom! No ma'am.

- **Tabitha Brown**

There was a strategy used when the colonizers stole our ancestors from Africa: divide and conquer. They separated families and elevated and degraded individuals based on skin tone, body composition, appearance, and more. This was not by happenstance; it was a deliberate tactic to cultivate distrust, animosity, and hierarchy. The more we are divided, the more vulnerable we become to harm. This system is still alive and well today, especially in the workplace.

In 2013, Dr. Kecia Thomas coined "Pet to Threat" as a form of workplace racism. It is described as a phenomenon in which Black women are likable until they tap into their power and use their voices to advocate for equity and change. They are then viewed as a threat to the status quo and met with retaliation from the dominant group, diminished support from mentors and managers, and denial of access to growth opportunities within the organization (Reese, 2022). I love the fact that Dr. Thomas put a name to this phenomenon. I have experienced being the "pet" and the "threat." When we give words to our experiences, it enhances the realness of them. We are also less likely to internalize them as figments of our imagination. I have four additional beliefs to corroborate the "Pet to Threat" phenomenon based on my workplace experiences and those I have observed.

First, I want to deconstruct the process and reflect on its psychological impacts. As a Black woman who wants to thrive in the workplace, it may be reflexive to strive for the "pet" status and do everything possible not to be viewed as a threat. Please do not personalize this position as something that you can aspire to. Pet and threat are two sides of the same coin. Your position on the continuum of this phenomenon is not on you or us as Black women. It is beyond our control by design. Being treated as a "pet" or a "threat" is a form of exploitation and an attempt to force assimilation to the comfortable flavor of the day. Yes, I did say the comfortable flavor of the day because it changes. What is deemed cool and comfortable today may be considered offensive, mean, aggressive, or insubordination tomorrow, next month, or next year.

Second, as a Black woman, you are and will always be a threat to insecure, unwell, and small-minded individuals. Often, there is nothing that you can do or could have done differently. Your energy, grace, brilliance, fierceness, beauty, wisdom, and DNA put you in that category in utero. To those who truly see you, you are a valuable and respected human being. Individuals and leaders with good intentions will strive to advocate and support you in thriving in your authentic voice and skin. Those threatened by your presence, gifts, and position will try to find ways to devalue, minimize, and silence you.

AS A BLACK WOMAN, YOU ARE AND WILL ALWAYS BE A THREAT TO INSECURE, UNWELL, AND SMALL-MINDED INDIVIDUALS.

Third, being the "pet" or the one who receives preferential treatment is a sham. The goal is to deplete you of your resources, ideas, knowledge, and relationships by first making you feel like the "chosen one." Don't get me wrong, being a "pet" has its benefits on the surface. It may include a nice corner office, parking space up front, a photo on the wall or company website, a big salary, power, influence, and more. Believe me, many less desirable things are going on behind the public curtains. Everything that glitters isn't gold. In the favorable "pet" position, I have been expected and asked to speak on behalf of all Black people. I've been asked if I knew someone who sold marijuana for a friend who was coming to town. I've navigated racism, microaggressions, fraudulent requests, ostracizing, and more. Above all the material things, it's the cost for me. The cost of harming myself and others. The cost of my soul and values in exchange for goods, services, perks, and money. The unwritten expectations for the "pet" position. Expectations that you will be the one who upholds or facilitates collateral damage to others through manipulation, disseminating false hopes and toxic positivity, exploitation, and standing in solidarity with the harmful behaviors of others. Once your resources and influence are no longer needed or desired, or you get fed up and say no, you're done! And they are on to find their next "pet" person.

Additionally, in the "Pet to Threat" phenomenon, pet and threat are two positions that are synonymous with the good and bad characters in a movie. The difference is when the movie ends, the characters return to their real identities, unimpacted by what occurred during their scenes. However, in the workplace, it's a continuous cycle of abuse and trauma. Unless we acknowledge its presence, refuse to participate, and take action to prioritize our well-being, it will continue to occur and cause harm.

Soul Compass

What is your workplace experience with the "Pet to Threat" phenomenon? If you are currently navigating it, how are you being perceived as the pet or threat?

The Black Confidant

No person is your friend who demands your silence or denies your right to grow.

- **Alice Walker**

"You're different from the others."

"I've never met anyone like you before."

Have you ever heard these statements? In my experience, sometimes, these statements are compliments, and sometimes, they are not. Sometimes, they are forms of gaslighting, microaggressions, nice racism, and tools of manipulation. It is important to make it your business to decipher, discern, and identify the roots of these statements and the intentions behind them to minimize harm. Sometimes, we feel honored when someone in a higher role comes to us for feedback on a challenging situation. We feel honored that the person thought highly of us and our expertise and felt "safe" in being vulnerable with us.

Yes, you are excellent in your own right by virtue of your Creator, DNA, hard work, expertise, personality, and more. However, you are not an anomaly of Black excellence. There are multitudes of Black women and men doing amazing things in their households, communities, workplaces, and the world daily. So when I hear someone say, "You are not like the others," I am no longer impressed. It's actually an insult and a bright red flag. Frequently, they don't personally know any other Black women. So it's not hard to be unique when there are no comparisons or when the comparisons are based on obnoxious reality television characters.

Additionally, I have found that unless the individual just dropped in from outer space or God recently changed their heart and opened their eyes, there were other Black women in their past. What happened to their relationships with those Black women? What role did they play in those relationships? Be diligent and curious in seeking the truth before you put your heart into this type of relationship. Before you get too excited, take a step back and get a bird's eye view of the situation and the individual. Here are some reflection questions.

- What's really occurring?

- What are this person's expectations of you and your responses?

- Why did they select you?

- Is the individual seeking a buddy to engage in uncomfortable and authentic conversations?

- Are they seeking strategies for their improvement? Or are they seeking someone to agree with them in reinforcing injustices, inequities, and abuse?

I have seen and experienced the Black confidant role play out very poorly in the workplace, most often around topics related to racism, whiteness culture, oppression, and privilege. One of the most frequent occurrences that I have witnessed is when a Black or Brown person calls out a white-bodied person for a harmful statement or action. Instead of leaning in, asking curious questions to that person, and taking steps to improve, the individual seeks comfort and validation of their actions from another Black woman, their Black confidant. This creates a "good" versus "bad" Black woman binary in the workplace. It also encourages an environment that lacks accountability and boundaries. The individual should be redirected to the original source of the disagreement whenever possible.

If we are unaware of when this is occurring and do not address it immediately, it will result in separation and division among Black women and their colleagues. It will cultivate an environment where the "good" employees try to maintain their "good" or "pet" or "Black confidant" status by any means necessary, while the "bad" employees are seen as a "threat" and are demonized, shunned, bullied, or terminated. Neither group talks to each other as a result of distrust, and both groups are ultimately being oppressed and abused, albeit in different ways.

This is in no way insinuating that being in a confidant relationship leads to bad outcomes 100% of the time. My point is that if it is not rooted in good intentions, it will lead to bad outcomes and harm. When there are good intentions, self-work, healthy boundaries, and accountability, things can go very well. The relationship must also be mutually beneficial emotionally and psychologically. I am blessed to have close relationships with women and men of various backgrounds, cultures, and races. These relationships are built on mutual trustworthiness, respect, authenticity, love, healthy boundaries, and accountability. It works because we hold ourselves and each other accountable to lifelong learning, curiosity, and reciprocity, and we lean into discomfort. The relationship does not require us to dance to find the right words to say. I can just be me; the other person can be their authentic self. This type of relationship requires strong muscles, and each person must be committed to building their muscles. The muscle is built through self-work, self-reflection, accountability, advocacy, action, and more. Weak muscles cannot hold heavy conversations. It's like trying to drive a car on four flat tires. Good luck with that!

Soul Compass

Have you ever been in the role of the Black confidant? What was this experience like for you? What sends up your red flag when it comes to this type of relationship? What constitutes a good and mutually beneficial relationship?

The Black Seat at the Table

Never beg for a seat when you can build your own table.

- Larenz Tate

Musical chairs is a game we played as kids. The game began with chairs being placed in an outward-facing circle. The number of chairs matched the number of participants. Someone played a song and randomly pressed pause to stop the music. Each time the music stopped, the participants had to rush to find an open seat and sit down. One chair would then be removed from the circle, and the music restarted. Participants who could not find a seat in time would be eliminated from the game. As the number of available seats dwindled, the participants would run, shove one another, and end up sitting on a portion of a chair or in someone's lap to try to garner a seat. This process would continue for several rounds until two participants and one seat remained. The participant who sat in the last seat won the game.

The musical chair model also shows up in organizations, especially when we are determined to gain or fight over what we perceive as the last seat or the only Black seat at the table. In many organizations, very few leadership positions are occupied by Black women. According to the 2023 Women in the Workplace Report, women of color represent 10% of senior management/director roles, compared to 16% of men of color, 27% of White women, and 49% of White men occupying these roles. Furthermore, the report indicates that for every 100 times a man is promoted to manager, Black women are promoted 54 times, Asian women 89 times, Latina women 76 times, and White women 91 times (Field et al., 2023). This exacerbates the challenges associated with the scarcity of these roles. It is important to remember there's no scarcity in Black brilliance and thriving. There's no need to fight one another for a seat at anyone's table. We have created and contributed to developing and enhancing many tables and seats. We are more than capable of creating our own. The system of racism was designed to perpetuate desensitization, division, devaluing, and destruction. It was designed to make us believe there is one or a minimal number of Black seats at the table. The goal is that this will incentivize us to fight one another for that one seat. Resist the urge to participate in this behavior.

THERE'S NO NEED TO FIGHT ONE ANOTHER FOR A SEAT AT ANYONE'S TABLE.

Our division is exacerbated when we judge one another against the everchanging white supremacy-influenced standards in our society. We internalize these harmful standards and make judgments of other individuals based on their personality, hairstyles, clothing, language, education, job title, life experiences, neighborhood, and much more. Based on these standards, we other those who do not "measure up." Once someone has been othered, it's easier to devalue them as mothers, siblings, friends, team members, leaders, and human beings. Devaluing someone enables us to erase aspects of their humanity. Devaluing often comes with labels. Labels like ghetto, mean, crazy, lazy, uneducated, aggressive, and more. Resist the urge to participate in this behavior. Next comes the destruction. This includes physical and emotional harm, such as the use of one's power, position, politics, and influence to further oppress, harm, or kill another human being. It also includes joining with others and supporting them in destroying others. This is not normal, and it is not okay.

Desensitization is a key ingredient of this process. It is the inability to sense or feel what another human being is experiencing and navigating. We must be able to feel one another. Not just imagining what it's like to walk in someone else's shoes but deeply feeling their experiences. It's empathy squared. This requires discomfort, self-awareness, and interrogating our privileges and power. Some say this is impossible, and I agree it is impossible to feel 100% of what another human being is navigating in their skin. However, I have seen people take the time to feel what infants, cats, dogs, plants, and mammals are experiencing and adjust their behaviors accordingly to contribute to positive outcomes.

Therefore, I believe we should also have the same capacity to do and be better to our fellow human beings.

Now, how does desensitization get reinforced? I believe through television and media. These elements are perpetuated by Black women on television shows, social media, and music repeatedly. Black women fighting while on vacation. Black women fighting in the workplace. Black women in stereotypical roles. I believe the goal is that we, as Black women, will absorb this foolishness and, in turn, will create and uphold harmful hierarchies among ourselves based on income, education, titles/roles, neighborhood, house size, skin tone, body and hair type, and more.

I've watched very intentionally, and I have not seen these things playing out in media for other races, ethnicities, and cultures in the same manner as it does for Black women. The behavior is immediately deemed a deviant anomaly when other groups "act the fool" in the media. The material is considered fake entertainment, and the individuals are categorized as acting. However, when it comes to Black women, words such as fake and entertaining are often thrown out of the window. These behaviors become character-defining moments and stereotypical reinforcements of who we are and how we interact with one another. These moments subconsciously become matter-of-fact; they will infiltrate our thoughts, beliefs, and interactions if we are not careful. Why does this type of media garner millions of dollars annually? Why is it on the backs of our Black women, girls, and communities? Who really benefits from this? I can tell you who is not benefiting from it: us!

We should occupy high-level executive leadership seats everywhere and in every industry. Why are we only allotted one or disproportionately few seats? Why are more seats not being brought to the table when we are highly qualified? Why is the executive leadership team not reconfiguring the current model to ensure equitable representation? This system was intentionally designed to make us think that we need to fight each other for that one Black seat at the table. As a result, we fight each other for it like it's the last seat in life, a badge of honor, or a signal that we've "arrived." The question is, arrived where? Ultimately, none of us are better off than the other. If we really knew how brilliant we are and the brilliance of our elders and ancestors, we could better embrace the fact that we built many of those chairs, tables, rooms, and more. And because we built them, we have the genius to create them again and again for ourselves and future generations. We can build them in our own movements or organizations, or organizations led by someone who respects, values, and appreciates us as human beings in our authentic skin.

Beautiful Black queens, we are stronger together. Unlearning division and competitiveness requires continuous self-reflection and practice. It requires acknowledging their origin, presence, and beneficiaries and taking positive action to rewrite the narrative daily. It will feel awkward at first, but keep practicing and doing it authentically until it becomes a natural part of who you are and how you navigate the world. I believe in you. I believe in the power of our U-N-I-T-Y.

Soul Compass

Does your organization have a Black seat(s)? If so, who currently holds the Black seat(s) at your organization's table? If you occupy this position, what has this experience been like for you?

CHAPTER 5
GETTING RELATIONSHIPS RIGHT

Skin Folk and Kinfolk

I am not free while any woman is unfree, even when her shackles are very different from my own.

- Audre Lorde

I can sense the virtual "whatabouts" coming up. There's a saying that all skin folk ain't kinfolk. This means everyone who looks like you may not have your best interest at heart. There is undeniable truth to this statement. There are many instances of us fighting against one another historically, and we can see it multiplied significantly today as it plays out in media, politics, religion, business, the workplace, and more. These types of systems have been created specifically for the purpose of division, manipulation, oppression, and exploitation. The more we separate and oppress ourselves, the less work the system has to do.

THE MORE WE SEPARATE AND OPPRESS OURSELVES, THE LESS WORK THE SYSTEM HAS TO DO.

Navigating workplace harm that is initiated or exacerbated by Black women is not something that I have experienced extensively. However, I would be remiss not to elevate the numerous real stories I have heard from Black and Brown women on how they have experienced significant workplace abuse and trauma that was led or exacerbated by Black and Brown women. Like anyone else and every group of people, we are not a monolith. Some Black women do not operate with the best of intentions and actions when it comes to other Black women, period. This can be caused by many things—for example, if we are striving to gain or maintain that mythical Black seat at the table, to maintain a "pet" status by any means necessary, to navigate self-hate on our journey to self-love, or to heal from things that made us feel lesser in our skin. It is unfortunate and inevitable that people will get hurt in the process.

As Black women, some of us see more examples of toxic relationships than healthy ones due to the media. However, some of us have intentionally disrupted negative generational patterns related to healthy relationships. Some of us are blessed to be surrounded by healthy relationships among

Black women. Some of us cling to our muscle memories of the beautiful and real friendships that our Big Momma and Granny cultivated during their lifetimes. Although distrust and maliciousness among Black women are over-indexed and exacerbated in our society, they are not unique to Black women. Toxic relationships occur across all races, genders, and cultures. Still, they are not portrayed and capitalized on in the same manner. However, I can honestly say it hits way harder when a Black woman facilitates harm to another Black woman. As a person who navigates racism, inequities, and injustices, there's a feeling that one should know better. They should understand better than participating in the same harm that has harmed them. In return, we become hypersensitive and build walls of resistance to protect ourselves.

Let me emphasize something: I am not saying that all Black women need to run out and become besties with the first Black woman they see. That would be reckless. However, I encourage you to be intentional and open to cultivating healthy relationships with other Black women. Systemic racism and oppression feed on our fighting, division, and isolation. Let's lean into our brilliance and rewrite our own stories. Walls keep us in and others out. Gates enable us to enter and exit to explore the possibilities and opportunities around us. Gates also allow us to let great people in and release those who are not such a great fit for our lives in a particular season. I have had the painful but necessary endeavor of having to release unhealthy relationships. That's life. Simultaneously, I have been abundantly blessed and honored to have crossed paths with countless phenomenal Black women throughout my life. Please do not allow fear, stereotypes, or past experiences to prevent you from meeting and gaining a fabulous Sista Friend with whom you can grow, learn, laugh, and celebrate together.

Soul Compass

How would creating a healthy and mutually beneficial relationship with a Black woman look, feel, and sound? What could you all achieve?

Everyone Can't Go Everywhere In Every Season

As your life evolves, so should your circle.

- Izey Victoria Odiase

When I was much younger, I remember becoming friends with people with similar hobbies and interests or, most of the time, individuals who shared similar classes. I am not sure how it occurred, but my childhood friends always had access to great food (fried fish and cheese grits, collard greens), desserts (cupcakes, sweet potato pies, pound cake, honey buns), or candy (banana-flavored Now and Laters, Sugar Daddies, Johnny Appleseed, Red Hots, Lemonheads). My friends and I laughed a lot and pulled lots of pranks on one another and other people. Those friendships were based on food, fun, and having a great time together. It was great and much needed in that season of my life.

However, just as seasons change, so do we as human beings, hopefully for the better. As I matured in the area of relationships, I realized that I needed much more. I love eating, laughing, and having fun like most people, but that is the icing on the cake for me. It is not the core of my being, mission, or purpose in life. As I continue to learn, grow, and evolve in this area, I realize I need to surround myself with people who have the capacity and desire to support and nourish the core parts of my being and becoming, as I also reciprocate this for them. Lord knows I've had more than my share of picking the wrong people in various seasons of my life. At the same time, I refuse to beat myself up about it, have a poor me pity party, or allow myself to be debilitated by it. Instead, I dusted myself off and hopped back on the trail. I took time to examine and learn from my relationship experiences. As I began to reflect, these experiences pointed back to me and my discernment, selection skills, and overriding subtle warning behaviors. I was then able to take the lessons I learned and create a plan to be and do better in this area of my life.

Our relationships impact our lives, journeys, goals, and outcomes. The impact can be positive or negative, and many times, the impact will make a lasting impression on our lives. This is why it is important to be intentional about whom we interact with and their position in our relational stratosphere.

Regardless of race, some individuals' interests are rooted in self and self-gratification by any means necessary. Some individuals' interests are rooted in great intentions but are unaligned with their actions. This way of being is a learned behavior and often comes along with being an imperfect and traumatized human being. In relationships, when an individual has unreconciled hurt, it increases their chances of causing harm when interacting with others, whether intentional or not. It is an indication that an individual needs to do a little more self-reflection, self-work, unlearning, relearning, and healing to be a better friend, colleague, associate, neighbor, businessperson, CEO, or other defined role.

OUR RELATIONSHIPS IMPACT OUR LIVES, JOURNEYS, GOALS, AND OUTCOMES.

Through my work as a national consultant, coach, and healing circle facilitator, I have met many people who have been emotionally debilitated by their relationships. As a result, they have leaned into fear and isolation as a form of self-protection. This seems to be multiplied significantly when it comes to Black women being in relationships with other Black women, especially after being harmed in a prior relationship with a Black woman. Yes, it hurts beyond what words can articulate to be harmed by a Black woman. However, it should not be a generalized indicator to be fearful of cultivating meaningful relationships with all Black women. Assess the situation, identify and learn the lessons, engage in healing yourself, and move forward.

Sometimes, we must interact sparingly and love people from afar. Sometimes, we must fully let go of the relationship and go our separate ways and love from a distance. Even if the relationship dissolves, we can still pray for them and desire for them to be their best self and succeed in life. Why is this such a big deal? Because division and animosity weaken us.

It is imperative that each of us identify our self-work in our relationships. This often means we must improve our people assessment and discernment skills. Not in a way that it feels like an interrogation to others, but in an intentional and unrushed manner. Getting to know people takes time. We also need to know ourselves and what we seek in a relationship with others. We need to know where we are heading, or at least the general direction. Creating standards for how we expect others to be and behave without first understanding ourselves, our needs, our boundaries, and what we are willing to contribute is a recipe for a toxic rollercoaster relationship. Friendships require nurturing, just like our other relationships.

Healthy relationships are necessary for our growth into the best versions of ourselves. I know this is possible. I have been blessed to have the honor of facilitating healing circles for Black women. The honor to watch mindsets and spaces transform as a result of Black women leaning into the discomfort of being vulnerable and open to healthy relationships and bravely rewriting the narrative around Black sisterhood. Life is done best with good relationships. The absence of this dampens our power and ability to be our greatest selves and reach our highest potential. We are stronger together. We possess the power to write our stories on how Black sisterhood looks, feels, and sounds. Let's go!

Soul Compass

Where are you heading? What characteristics would be most helpful for you in this season of your life? What does that look like in another human being?

CHAPTER 6
LIFE JACKETS

The goal of section one was to define Rough S.E.A.S. and provide an overview of how they show up in the workplace and their impacts on our power, wellness, and joy. The purpose of the Life Jackets subsection is to provide a summary of quick tips for common challenges. Life jackets are things that we can quickly apply to support us and help us float and breathe in the midst of the rough waves.

LIFE JACKETS ARE THINGS THAT WE CAN QUICKLY APPLY TO SUPPORT US AND HELP US FLOAT AND BREATHE IN THE MIDST OF THE ROUGH WAVES.

- **Challenge: Jumping in headfirst with your eyes closed.**

    - Open your eyes. It's important for you to fully see, hear, feel, and experience the workplace culture surrounding you. Pay attention to the silence and spoken words. Understand the players and the games being played; there is always a game being played.

- **Challenge: Knowing the experiences of others but thinking it will be different for you.**

    - Like a well-oiled merry-go-round, your turn is coming. It may be next quarter, next year, or a few years from now. You are not an exception. There is no dipping and ducking in a toxic workplace culture.

- **Challenge: Being a magical Black woman confidant.**

    - Understand the intent, goals, and expectations of the other person. Understand your expectations and intentions as well. What are the costs, and what are the benefits? Is this type of relationship good for your soul and emotional well-being?

- **Challenge: Thinking what you are feeling or observing is not real.**

  - Trust your intuition and believe what you see, hear, and feel. It is not your imagination, and you are not exaggerating or being overly critical. Trust yourself to know what helps and what harms you.

- **Challenge: Believing you are alone.**

  - You may be the only one or one of a few in your workplace, but please know other women are experiencing Rough S.E.A.S. in their workplaces, too. If they are not currently experiencing Rough S.E.A.S., there's a great chance that they have experienced them in the past.

- **Challenge: Staying and fighting everything in sight.**

  - This is exhausting and harmful. Practice being strategic in what and how you fight. Partner with other workplace advocates (internal and external) to share the weight. This pathway will also enable you to establish room for breaks and breaths. You don't have to speak at all times. There is power in your silence.

- **Challenge: Contorting yourself to make others feel more comfortable in your presence.**

  - Don't allow someone else's insecurities, fragility, and power thirst to burden you and twist you like a pretzel. Take a step back, breathe, and allow others to do their work. Focus on being the best version of yourself. If you are not you, who will you be? Stand tall and resist the urge to conform to harmful ways of being. People eat pretzels as snacks.

- **Challenge: Allowing imposter syndrome to keep you bound to a job or position that is harming you.**

  - No one intentionally hires someone who doesn't bring value. You were hired because of your current and future excellence. Your job did not make you excellent. Your job is merely a platform for exploring and sharing your gifts with others. Imposter syndrome is often a byproduct of not seeing anyone who looks like you excelling in your role, workplace, or industry. It is important to surround yourself with leaders who look like you. This is one of the many benefits of being in a community with other Black and Brown leaders.

- **Challenge: Overriding your breaking point.**

  - Overriding or not knowing your breaking point exacerbates harm and traumas. Know when it's your time to go before the locks are changed. The locks can be changed due to termination, physical or emotional illnesses, burnout, or other reasons. Prioritize yourself and your well-being, health, and joy.

- **Challenge: Conflating your purpose with a platform.**

  - Many times, we become one with our jobs. Our job becomes what we hold on to because we are doing what we love and were created to do there. We were born with our purpose. A job is one of thousands of platforms used to disseminate goods and services. The organization can go out of business tomorrow, but that doesn't stop your purpose. The purpose train has already left the station!

- **Challenge: Being grateful isn't a pass for abuse.**

  - Two things can be true: you can be grateful for a job, benefits, and a paycheck and simultaneously be frustrated, exhausted, and traumatized by your job. Being grateful does not require complacency with workplace abuse. Prioritize your peace, wellness, and joy. Reclaim your power. Find the spaces that celebrate you and your authenticity.

- **Challenge: Depending on others to be okay with you leaving or staying.**

  - You are the only person who knows what it's like to be you. Only you can determine your tipping point. When it comes to the costs versus benefits of working in an organization, you decide whether or not you leave or stay. If you believe in the power of prayer, pray for the wisdom to know when to stay and when to leave, a great support system, the courage to take action, favor, and an illuminated path.

CHAPTER 7

THE SEVEN WAVES OF ROUGH S.E.A.S. NAVIGATION TOOL ™

Many models describe phases and behaviors associated with abuse from the lens of the person inflicting the abuse. There are notably fewer models that outline the phases and stages of abuse from a survivor's lens and even fewer related to workplace abuse and trauma from a survivor's lens. I believe it is vital to highlight the effects of workplace abuse and trauma and the stages experienced by individuals who are navigating this.

The Seven Waves of Rough S.E.A.S.™ is a model that highlights the phases of emotions employees navigate in the workplace. The model offers an impact continuum based on positive and negative experiences in the workplace. When utilized as an individual tool, it allows individuals to locate themselves on a wave. When utilized as an organizational tool, leaders can graphically observe the aggregated wave trends among their employees. It is important to note that assessments are a snapshot in time. An individual's waves can change over time depending on their experiences with the organization. This can be positive or negative, depending on the circumstances. Therefore, it is recommended that the tool be facilitated annually, at a minimum.

The most important thing to note is that leaders can positively change how their employees experience the organization, beginning with this tool and strategic action steps. LEIDOSWEL offers learning experiences through consulting, coaching, and training that assist organizations in becoming unstuck and thriving. Additional information regarding our individual, group, and organizational learning experiences can be found in the About LEIDOSWEL™ section of the book. An overview of the model and a brief description of the waves are shared below.

Figure 1
The Seven Waves of Rough S.E.A.S.

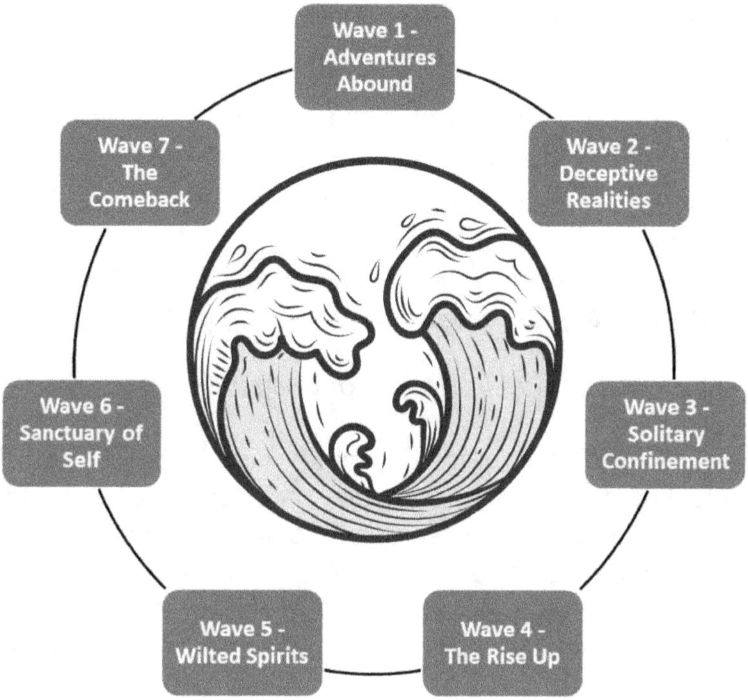

- Wave 1 - Adventures Abound
- Wave 2 - Deceptive Realities
- Wave 3 - Solitary Confinement
- Wave 4 - The Rise Up
- Wave 5 - Wilted Spirits
- Wave 6 - Sanctuary of Self
- Wave 7 - The Comeback

Note. By Freeman-Foster, T. (2023). Copyright by LEIDOSWEL™

Wave 1 - Adventures Abound

Themes: *Exploration, Honeymooning, and Imperfect Harmony*

Human Experience: As a new or long-term employee, things at the organization are going well. The organization's culture and climate are in alignment with its mission, vision, and values. The organization is imperfect, but its leaders and team members value and respect each other and work together to solve problems.

Wave 2 - Deceptive Realities

Themes: *Shock, Denial, and Questioning*

Human Experience: A situation that does not align with the organization's stated values occurs. The employee analyzes the situation to determine the cause, intent, and organizational response. The employee may also begin the process of assessing their fit with the organization.

Wave 3 - Solitary Confinement

Themes: *Questioning, Isolation, and Guilt*

Human Experience: More situations unaligned with the organization's stated values are occurring with little to no response from the leadership to explain the causes or action steps to solutions. The employee is assessing the depth of the situation while feeling guilty for thinking negatively about the organization and begins to insulate themselves to process things at a deeper level.

Wave 4 - The Rise Up

Themes: *Advocacy, Shame, and Anger*

Human Experience: The employee musters up the courage to speak up and advocate for a better working environment or solution to the challenges. They are met with othering, silence, inaction, gaslighting, or other retaliation. If the impact of the culture was not already personal, it has become personal for the employee.

Wave 5 - Wilted Spirits

Themes: *Exhaustion, Depression, and Detachment*

Human Experience: The employee feels defeated. They find ways to remove themselves from as many spaces as possible to maintain distance from the offending team members. The employee is also struggling internally to reconcile the misalignment between the organization's stated values and actual values and how these intersect with the employee's personal values.

Wave 6 - Sanctuary of Self

Theme: *Emotional Respite and Self-Preservation*

Human Experience: The employee is focused on survival. They have come to terms with the organization maintaining its current stance. They may find solitude and mutual support in internal or external spaces with individuals who understand or those who are experiencing the organization similarly. The employee is developing a plan of action that consists of a plan to protect their wellness, exit the organization, or both.

Wave 7 - The Comeback

Themes: *Healing and Reclamation of Self*

Human Experience: The employee separates the purpose from the platform. They are focused on learning from the experience, immersing themselves in supportive and therapeutic spaces and places, and restoring themselves to the best version of themselves.

About the Waves

Now that you have a greater understanding of the model and the waves, let's discuss the intention and the flow of the waves. The Seven Waves of Rough S.E.A.S. Navigation Tool provides categories of phases that employees may experience as they are navigating workplace trauma and abuse. The model is not indicative of every emotion, as that would be impossible.

However, the themes were created broadly with the goal of aiding individuals in locating themselves. If people can locate where they are, they are more likely to engage the resources and skills necessary to pivot to a healthier space that supports them in becoming unstuck physically, emotionally, and spiritually.

The model was intentionally created with the waves being connected but not dependent on one another. It is an individual experience with collective themes. While there is often a dominant wave, individuals may experience multiple waves simultaneously, independently, sequentially, or nonconsecutively. The waves are influenced by where the person was emotionally prior to the situation, the actual situation, and the roles and behaviors of the persons involved. Here are a few examples:

1. If an individual is navigating challenges and traumas external to the workplace, such as challenges with their parents, significant other/spouse, children, or another loved one, it becomes difficult to focus on navigating and healing their workplace trauma.

2. Ongoing challenges and traumas within the same workplace or previous workplaces contribute to weathering. If an individual is already navigating or healing from past workplace traumas, they are most likely extremely vulnerable, so the current workplace trauma creates a compound and even more damaging effect.

3. Mental health conditions unrelated, caused, or exacerbated by their workplace experiences may create barriers to effectively navigating workplace abuse and trauma. It may also blur an individual's ability to see a positive way out of the situation.

4. Research studies demonstrate the harmful effects of being the only Black woman in leadership at an organization.

Having an ally or someone within the organization to support and lead the advocacy for change makes a huge difference. It ensures the weight is shared and shifted when needed. It also provides opportunities to cultivate spaces to vent and have solutions-focused conversations.

5. External communities provide a space for individuals with similar mindsets, skills, interests, or aspirations to support one another. These spaces can be virtual or in-person and can be based on emotional, spiritual, physical, or social wellness activities. These communities serve as a protective factor.

6. This book encourages readers to develop a pivot plan. There is something extremely powerful about having an actionable plan at your fingertips. Having a plan helps individuals become unstuck and gives them the confidence necessary to take healthy actions.

It is important to keep in mind that Rough S.E.A.S. —Soul Eroding Assimilation-Forcing Systems can be extremely dangerous regardless of the waves an individual is navigating. Each wave should be taken seriously. Just as waves in an ocean, the intensity of the wave can have and contribute to life-threatening outcomes, chronic illness, suicidal ideations and attempts, and premature death. This should create a crisis-level response. Individuals experiencing Rough S.E.A.S. should seek emotional support immediately. Organizations contributing to Rough S.E.A.S. need to seek external and internal support and develop actionable strategies to improve the workplace culture immediately.

Click here to access your FREE Seven Waves of Rough S.E.A.S. Navigation Quiz https://bit.ly/7WavesOfRoughSeas.

SECTION 02

A NAVIGATOR'S MINDSET

The goal of this section of the book is to advance from drowning or struggling at sea to becoming empowered and confident at sea. This is an awakening.

Congratulations! Your vision is unobstructed, and you have clarity. You realize the realness of your situation and understand its impacts. The next step is taking action that leads to purposeful success. This requires doing the work to move from emotionally drowning in your workplace to implementing actions to take your power back and actively protect your wellness and joy.

Section two is dedicated to developing the tools, mindset, skillset, and community necessary to become a navigator. This section is devoted to strategies. It will require leaning in, interrogating, and unlearning messaging that no longer serves us well and replacing it with new things that support our thriving. It will also require an abundance of love and grace for ourselves and patience with the process. These virtues are most powerful when paired with accountability. We must hold ourselves accountable for doing our work, not give up, and surround ourselves with individuals who can support us. Some days, we will be navigators, and some days, something random will occur, and we will find ourselves struggling to make it through a moment, day, or week. However, this should not stop us from aspiring to a navigator's mindset every day. It's a lifelong journey and not a sprint. Remember, you deserve joy, wellness, peace, prosperity, and more!

THE ALARM SOUNDS!

Panic buttons are pressed. The alarm sounds. Screams of *run, run, run!* are ringing out. Personnel files are pulled. Employee handbooks are opened. Next are closed doors, selective group texts, video or phone calls, emails, and lunchtime and after-hours conversations. People are experiencing discomfort. Power is being challenged. Silence is now sound. People are being called in. The status quo is being called out.

What happened? A Black woman used her power to speak up and take action, and the world shifted!

Dr. Tonicia Freeman-Foster

CHAPTER 8
GET YOUR MIND RIGHT

Assess Your Bag

Bag Lady, you gon' miss your bus. You can't hurry up 'cause you got too much stuff.

- Erykah Badu

The first step in a navigator's mindset journey is cleansing our mental and emotional scripts. Unpacking our suitcases, as I often say. If you are a traveler, you are most likely aware of the baggage check process. When traveling by airplane or ship, passengers must have their bags assessed. This security measure is implemented to ensure your safety and that of others. Imagine what could occur if this measure were not in place. Imagine the items that could cause harm to yourself or other passengers. There are things that we use on land every day, such as lithium batteries, that may not fare well when placed in a pressurized cabin. This rule applies to our lives as well. Some people are phenomenal when things are stable in our lives, and some specialize in hard times and crises. However, these individuals may or may not be as effective when it comes time for us to fly to the next level of our purpose or when we begin to experience turbulence while in flight. This is why we must continually assess our relationships and ensure the right people are on our plane and in the right seats on our plane. This also applies to messaging. There are things we were told or learned that carried us through a particular situation or season in our lives. They may have been effective then, but these messages are no longer effective at this age, stage, and season of our lives.

I believe each of us has a suitcase or bag that we inherited at birth. We carry it with us as we move throughout the world each day. Our bags contain artifacts of our lived and inherited life experiences. They contain words, actions, and things we have experienced and been told by our friends, family, loved ones, associates, random strangers, haters, and foes. They contain experiences and things we learned in social circles, religious institutions, and media. Our bags also contain our workplace experiences and messaging regarding how we should show up in the workplace and "behave" as Black women. Although we try to focus on our positive experiences, achievements, words, and accolades, the negative ones also find their way into our suitcases and bags. If we are not careful, they will manifest themselves through emotional, mental, and physical illness.

They will cause us to doubt ourselves and our excellence and diminish our confidence in our ability to achieve our dreams and goals. We may also begin to feel like imposters, which sets us on a slippery slope downward. We must disrupt this process.

THE NEGATIVE EXPERIENCES WE TAKE TO HEART AND NEVER LET GO OF IMPOSE THE MOST WEIGHT ON OUR MINDS, BODIES, AND SOULS.

The negative experiences we take to heart and never let go of impose the most weight on our minds, bodies, and souls. Imagine that your mind, body, and soul are bags and suitcases. Some of our bags are carry-on-sized suitcases, others are large, and others have exceeded the maximum weight limit to the point that we can't even pay a fee to obtain boarding approval. Some are too heavy to manage on our own, so we prop and store them in various locations because they have become too heavy to move. I get it. I get wanting to prop and leave your suitcase somewhere and return to it later. The problem is when we use it as a form of escapism to the point where we never take the time to assess and unpack its contents. And we only see our suitcase when we open it to add more stuff. We cannot afford to do this. Our purpose is too great. These oversized, heavy, and immobile suitcases will cause us to miss our opportunity flights if left unaddressed and unhealed.

Today, I claim we will not miss any more opportunity flights. We will not miss opportunities to enjoy the adventures of life that make our hearts smile. We will not miss the opportunities to immerse ourselves in things we were created to do and become because our bags are too heavy. We will seek, assertively request, and obtain the therapy, support, and services necessary for our thriving. I can believe this for you and us, but it will not make a difference if you don't believe it is possible. Do you believe this for yourself? Are you ready? If so, please join me in the process of unpacking. Let's start by opening our bag or suitcase, assessing its contents, and inspecting every compartment.

Soul Compass

What's in your bag? How are these things impacting your work and personal life?

Download the complimentary Navigating Rough S.E.A.S. workbook to learn more about assessing your suitcase:

http://www.navigatingroughseasworkbook.com.

Unpack Your Bag

Your willingness to look at your darkness is what empowers you to change.

- Iyanla Vanzant

Can you imagine being on an airplane without luggage weight restrictions? Would you feel safe? I wouldn't. More than likely, I would figure out another method for getting to my destination, even if it took longer to get there. Unfortunately, our minds don't come with luggage scales. How cool would it be to have a baggage checker that warned us that we were nearing our unique weight capacity before our minds and bodies became overwhelmed? Humans are blessed with the ability to reason and draw inferences from our experiences. The challenge is when we override the subtle warning signs, and those little signs grow into bigger signs. We then begin to progress into the areas that cause and exacerbate our hurt, harm, and collateral damage to others.

Unpacking our bag requires self-awareness and self-reflection. It requires courage to interrogate what we have learned throughout our lives and unlearn the things that no longer or have never served us well. Things that have resulted in generalizations, untruths, and the oppression of ourselves and others. This includes messaging rooted in fear instead of fierceness, faulty religious messaging, poor assessments of ourselves, false narratives of past events, and other harmful messaging. It also includes assimilation-forcing messaging. Messaging that tells us that we need to be, believe or behave in a manner that is inauthentic to who we were created to be.

Our experiences influence our beliefs, and our beliefs influence our actions. Unpacking our bags is one of the most challenging endeavors on this journey because it requires us to interrogate and unlearn harmful beliefs taught or modeled by people who love us. Generational belief and behavioral patterns are often rooted in fear, survival, and attempts to regain power and control over one's life and environment. Most times, people are doing their best. What would it feel like if we forgave them and moved forward instead of being upset and resentful?

Unpacking our bags is also one of the most challenging endeavors on this journey because it requires us to come face to face with the wise advisement and suggestions we received, disregarded, and overrode. Those messages could have saved us from heartache and harm. Don't beat yourself up about this. The good part is that you learned from your past mistakes, and if you had the chance to do it over again, you may do things differently. The not-so-good part is that life doesn't allow us to travel back in time; we can only go forward. However, the wisdom that we received is not lost. We can take that wisdom and the lessons learned, apply it to our lives going forward, and support others who may need our help and advice.

> **WE CAN TAKE THAT WISDOM AND THE LESSONS LEARNED, APPLY IT TO OUR LIVES GOING FORWARD, AND SUPPORT OTHERS WHO MAY NEED OUR HELP AND ADVICE.**

As you unpack your suitcase, remove the things that no longer or have never served you well. Identify the things, wise counsel, and lessons that will assist you in navigating this season of your life, and move them to the front of the suitcase. Resist the urge to overpack. Leave room for souvenirs and life gems you will gain through your experiences and interactions with others. The ultimate goal is that your suitcase should excite you. It should be filled with things that will serve you well. Things that will help you grow, challenge you, and support you in reaching your next destination. The baton has been passed to you. You have the power to change your trajectory and positively influence the lives of those around you. What are you going to do?

It begins with YOU loving and believing in yourself.

- You must believe you can and deserve to thrive.

- You must believe you were created to solve a problem in the world and that people are waiting for you, your authentic presence and voice.

- You must believe in the possibilities of your gifts and what can occur when you unleash the real and complete version of you!

- You must believe that you deserve to work in a place that actively prioritizes your health and well-being and avoids causing or contributing to harm and illness. Not just in spoken or written words but also through real actions. This may result in you creating this for yourself through your own business ventures. Even if you don't see entrepreneurship as your thing, that's okay; just be open to the possibilities.

- You must believe that you deserve and need to be in a community with others who can support you. A space or place where you are seen, heard, believed, valued, and celebrated as your entire, unapologetically authentic self.

- You must believe you are worth the work, time, and energy.

- You must believe in YOU!

Don't Dilute Your Sweet Tea

The graveyard is the richest place on the surface of the earth because there, you will see the books that were not published, ideas that were not harnessed, songs that were not sung, and drama pieces that were never acted.

- Dr. Myles Munroe

- If using your strength for good makes someone else feel weak, that's their stuff.

- If your courage to make a positive difference makes someone else feel afraid, that's their stuff.

- If being your brilliant, beautiful, and Black self intimidates others, that's their stuff.

Things are getting exciting! We have assessed and unpacked our bags. We are rolling and ready to explore our opportunity flights. What if I told you that your next great opportunity would require you to embrace and bring all of your wisdom, challenges, lessons learned, expertise, and lived experiences centered in your authentic voice, lenses, and uniqueness? What if I told you that your next great opportunity would value, celebrate, generously compensate, and honor all of these intersections? What would you do? How would you feel?

Identifying and remaining true to ourselves is the key to achieving our divine purpose. People are going to think and feel a myriad of ways about you. That does not mean you abandon your power and allow others to mold you into who and how they see, desire, or believe you should be. That's too much power to give away to someone else. That's God power. Not people power. If you know who you are and have at least a tiny idea of your purpose, you can resist being tempted to allow someone else to mold you. People can contribute to your life but should not attempt to change who you are to fulfill their needs, fears, and insecurities. All contributions should be well vetted. This will be discussed more in the next chapter.

Stand tall in who you are, whose you are, and who you are becoming, even when it feels uncomfortable. Give people their stuff back and allow them to do their own work. Do not ever allow anyone to make you feel small. Do not ever allow anyone to cause you to make yourself small. Besides, you're too tall to be small. Your light shines bright, and there is no dimmer.

There's someone who needs to see you use your power and authentically unleash your gifts because it gives them the courage to do the same. Be the light that illuminates their path.

THERE'S SOMEONE WHO NEEDS TO SEE YOU USE YOUR POWER AND AUTHENTICALLY UNLEASH YOUR GIFTS BECAUSE IT GIVES THEM THE COURAGE TO DO THE SAME.

Ready for some tea? I discussed tipping points in a prior chapter. Tipping points can yield positive or negative results. This proverbial ball rolls in both directions. Think about the process of making a glass of good sweet tea. There is a delicate yet unequal balance of three main ingredients: tea, sugar, and water. Depending on your geographic location and personal preferences, you may say that lemon or other ingredients also play a big part. If so, no offense or knock on your sweet tea recipe. For this demonstration, we will stick to the three ingredients previously mentioned.

The tea becomes too sweet to drink if too much sugar is added. If too much water is added, the tea becomes flat and bland. If not enough tea is added, it tastes like sugar water. The ingredients are not added in equal parts, but a specific balance is necessary to create good sweet tea. Depending on your preferred taste, there is usually one ingredient in a specific measurement that may elevate the taste to the next level for you.

A less-than-preferred outcome can also occur with our gifts and talents. Sometimes, we dilute our own sweet tea, especially when we drift from our purpose and authenticity. We dilute our skills and talents to make others feel good and comfortable with us through people-pleasing behaviors because we have lost our way or are trying to find our path to our purpose. Undoubtedly, we need people to be our best selves and reach our fullest potential. However, if we depend on people to tell us who they believe we are without first having at least a clue for ourselves, we become like a glass of diluted and bland tea. Everyone should not have access to or the ability to contribute or add things to your sweet tea. Open access allows everyone to take turns putting ingredients in the amounts they think are best. Some add more water, some add more sugar, some add more tea, and some experiment with random ingredients like cinnamon and peaches. We slowly lose sight of ourselves during this process, and our purpose becomes cloudy. This distracts from our impact. My motto is that if I could do five things great or ten things good, I would choose five things great. This would enable me to narrow down, relentlessly pursue, and immerse myself in learning and mastering the five selected things. I don't want to be known for doing a little bit of everything. I want to be known for doing a lot of my thing. The thing that I was created to do. The thing that ignites the change that I was created to make.

Soul Compass

What do you believe is the change that you were created to ignite? When will the world see it in its fullest?

Return Check to Sender

I have learned that as long as I hold fast to my beliefs and values - and follow my own moral compass - then the only expectations I need to live up to are my own.

- **Michelle Obama**

Protecting your mind is key to a navigator's mindset. Your mind serves as the front door to your body. Our mind is connected to our emotional, financial, physical, and spiritual thriving. The state of our mind determines whether we speak life or defeat to ourselves. Through our minds, we possess the shackles that keep us grounded and bounded or the power to unleash our fullest potential to thrive and soar like eagles.

Back in the day, there was a saying: *sticks and stones may break my bones, but words will never hurt me*. It sounded good, and it was powerful, especially when it was directed at a bully. However, as we mature, we realize that words have a great effect. And sometimes words hurt more than broken bones. Words have a way of staying in our brains and playing repeatedly like a scratched record long after broken bones have healed. Negative words have a way of showing up when we feel the most alone, overwhelmed, uncertain, stuck, and defeated. Words are seeds that grow into plants and multiply quickly. This is why it's super important to be intentional about who and what we surround ourselves with and the messaging we receive. The goal is to fill our brain with positive messaging to the point where it significantly outweighs, turns down the volume, and ultimately presses mute on the negative messaging. This requires consistency and action.

THE GOAL IS TO FILL OUR BRAIN WITH POSITIVE MESSAGING TO THE POINT WHERE IT SIGNIFICANTLY OUTWEIGHS, TURNS DOWN THE VOLUME, AND ULTIMATELY PRESSES MUTE ON THE NEGATIVE MESSAGING.

In the workplace, I use an approach I titled "return check to sender." Let's think about a banking transaction. If you were to take a check for a substantial amount written by a third party to the bank, the bank would place a hold on it before accepting it as a deposit. The check amount would determine the number of days for the hold placed on the transaction. Larger amounts may result in longer holds. Newer accounts may also result in longer holds. During the holding period, the bank would ensure the person or entity that wrote the check has enough money in their account to cover the check. This loss prevention strategy protects your bank and your account from being defrauded.

In my efforts to remain cognizant of the power of words at all times, I place holds on the advisements, recommendations, and requests of others before I allow their words to be planted and take root in my mental garden. During these holds, I interrogate the messaging to determine the intent. What are the messenger's goals? How was the information communicated, and what words did they use? Is the goal to support my growth and development or an attempt to force me to assimilate into an inauthentic version of myself to appease others? Is the intent to persuade me to assimilate into a culture that harms myself or others? I determine how to proceed based on my answers to these reflection questions. I determine if I will accept the entire deposit or a portion of it or reject it completely and return the check to the sender. This process helps me to guard my mind and protect myself against harmful messaging.

Here's an example. A supervisor once told me that a colleague and I were not getting along because the colleague probably felt bullied. If you know me well, you know I am intentional about the words I allow others to use when describing me. When I began asking clarifying questions, the response was that the colleague was intimidated by me because of my organizational skills and the level of work I facilitated to support my clients in achieving positive outcomes. It was that I "crossed all of my t's" and "dotted all of my i's." I was floored. Queens, this is not the definition of being a bully, and this was not my stuff. I immediately returned that check to the sender. Otherwise, I would have deposited that check and mulled over those words continuously. I would have personalized it, made it about me, and spent a significant amount of time trying to identify ways I could show up as less threatening or intimidating. I would have denied the other party the ability to sit with their discomfort and improve their skills. I would have also diverted time and energy away from my purpose and work and engaged in something irrelevant to me. This is why we cannot allow everyone to put their ingredients into our sweet tea. We must interrogate the narratives people tell us and attempt to place on us and be diligent about returning the check to the sender whenever it does not align with the truth.

Sometimes, we even have to protect our minds against our own negative self-talk. In these cases, the deposit must be interrogated to determine the original source. Who or what told you that about you? Why do you believe it? Once interrogated, the check must be thrown in the garbage and replaced with positive messaging. Do not get stuck keeping a check for days, months, or years. If you do, it will take root and become a script that plays repeatedly in your mind. Talk to yourself how you would want someone who deeply cares and loves you to speak to you. Anything less is completely unacceptable. If you struggle with this, obtaining a therapist, coach, or both may be great tools to support you.

Soul Compass

How do you guard your mind against the negative words of others? How do you talk to yourself? What practices have you implemented? How are they working for you?

CHAPTER 9
OPEN YOUR EYES

Forecasting Rain

A threat to injustice for one is a threat to injustice for all.

— **Dr. Martin Luther King, Jr.**

One of the best ways to navigate a toxic or abusive workplace is by first grounding ourselves in reality. We can pray and hope for something different, but we must first be real about the situation. Just because we desire something to be different does not make it that way. We can turn flips, tap our shoes together three times, and talk about it until our voice becomes hoarse, and things remain the same. We can be real and hopeful at the same time.

WE CAN PRAY AND HOPE FOR SOMETHING DIFFERENT, BUT WE MUST FIRST BE REAL ABOUT THE SITUATION.

It is important to avoid delusional romanticizing of the situation, or as I often say, putting frosting and sprinkles on rotten cake. As a consultant, this is a response that I have observed in many leaders. I am unsure if it's an effort to present the organization favorably to me, their ego, or a genuine detachment from what's occurring in their organization. Whatever the reason, the results are the same. Most people don't go around fixing things that are not broken. So, if there is a foundational belief that things are good, more than likely, no change will occur.

If something is bad or harmful, there's no changing the fact that it's bad or harmful. Let's call a spade a spade. For example, you can desire for it not to rain because you are about to attend your favorite outdoor concert. However, the weather woman forecasts rain. You look outside and notice it's getting cloudy. You can choose to ignore the forecast and storm clouds and leave home unprepared, or you can accept the reality that it may actually rain and prepare by taking your rain gear. Either way, there's a great chance that water will fall from the sky. It may not rain at all, it may rain for a quick moment, or it may rain throughout the entire concert. The question is, will you be prepared?

While we are on the subject of rain, there is an interesting phenomenon that I have observed in the workplace. I refer to it as the scattered showers approach to workplace harm and abuse. It occurs when someone watches it rain on someone else's street, and instead of preparing for the rain, they are praying and hoping that somehow the rain will skip over their street. Even if the rain skips your street today, it does not mean you are safe tomorrow, next week, next month, or next year. In my humble opinion and experience, if inequities and injustices happen to others within your workplace, you are not safe either. Prepare for the rain.

Soul Compass

What is the culture of your workplace? How are you experiencing it?

Promised Change

*I am no longer accepting the things
I cannot change. I am changing the things
I cannot accept.*

- **Angela Davis**

Promised change is a beast! I've had the unfortunate experience of waiting on promised change on more than one occasion. I have also had the unfortunate experience of watching other Black women wait for change that was promised by their organization's leadership to their own physical and emotional detriment. The absence of change is one thing. The promise of change that never occurs but is continually promised can be devastating. Individuals are subjecting themselves to harm in hopes that positive changes are around the corner if they just hold on a little longer. I have experienced this, and I would not wish this harm on anyone. In fact, I want to let you in on the game so you can be proactive in pivoting, allowing you to decrease or eliminate the impact of the harm.

It is a form of manipulation and exploitation when a leader intentionally lies and creates false hopes about changes they have the power to make and have no intention of implementing. Usually, it's connected to productivity, optics, and the organization's financial gain. The goal is that you will continue to work hard at the same level or higher, contributing to the organization's billing, funding, or image as you await the promised change. Simultaneously, you continue to navigate abuse and receive carrots to string you along. Here are a few carrots that I have heard about and observed.

- We are working on it.

- This is a large undertaking, and it will take some time.

- We are not sure where to begin in working on this.

- We will take it to the Board and get back to you.

- Can you write a brief statement so we can better understand the situation?

- This is important to us—thank you for your patience.

- More grace is needed; we all have things to work on.

- I feel harmed because of how you presented this. I need to sit with this and gather my thoughts.

Have you ever heard any of these statements? What actions were taken? What impact did those actions make in the workplace? I sincerely hope there was a quick response and a positive workplace impact.

On the contrary, if you've presented the problem and no positive and visible action has been taken, or if action was taken and not sustained, then more than likely, nothing impactful will happen. Inaction is action, too. It means someone chose not to address the harmful matter at hand. With the dangling carrot of change, something is always about to happen, but nothing significant ever happens. Do not allow people to waste your time, string you along, or gas you up by telling you they need additional time, money, people, or other resources. People make time and take meaningful action on things they deem important. People prioritize solutions to things they deem to be harmful to them. If the situation hasn't been prioritized, it probably hasn't been deemed important or harmful. As navigators, we must tell ourselves the truth. This is necessary for pivoting and planning our response. Create the change you wish to see.

> DO NOT ALLOW PEOPLE TO WASTE YOUR TIME, STRING YOU ALONG, OR GAS YOU UP BY TELLING YOU THEY NEED ADDITIONAL TIME, MONEY, PEOPLE, OR OTHER RESOURCES.

Soul Compass

What do you need to thrive at work? What does positive change look, sound, and feel like for you at your current organization?

What steps have you taken to gain the support you need, internally or externally?

Check Receipts

You don't have to live near me; just give me my share of equality.

- Nina Simone

During my master's degree program, I had an amazing professor for my program evaluation and sustainability course. What I loved the most was that he taught us not only various evaluation models but also practical applications and life lessons. One of the many things he taught us that resonates with me today is not to allow people to just tell you anything without producing data or other substantial materials to support their statements. This is the nice version of the lesson.

As I reflected on this lesson and pondered its connection to Rough S.E.A.S. —Soul Eroding Assimilation-Forcing Systems, the following thoughts came up for me. Change has receipts. When you purchase an item from a business, you receive a receipt or itemized record of the transaction. If you made the purchase in person and paid with cash, you also receive change. Any organization committed to change should be able to produce receipts. The receipts should demonstrate where the organization started, where it is headed, and where it is currently in the process. Change requires action. There should be evidence of actions that validate what they are saying. Lack of evidence or lack of substantial evidence is a red flag. Lack of clarity around the evidence is a red flag as well. If you start asking questions and people begin fumbling over their words, are unsure and need to ask someone else, or try to skate around your questions, these are red flags that change may not actually be occurring.

CHANGE HAS RECEIPTS.

Change should not be invisible. Change takes time, but there should be clear evidence of progress. Building a home takes time, but you can drive by and observe incremental progress being made on a daily or weekly basis. In an organization, everyone should be aware of the change plan and have a role in implementing or evaluating it. This includes administration, direct services, management, C-suite, board of directors, community members, clients, and vendors. Engaging others in the process ensures progress. Where there is a lack of progress, there will be a lack of positive change, and over time, previous efforts will begin to diminish or regress.

Soul Compass

Does your organization have receipts for the things it promises to provide? What do these receipts consist of?

CHAPTER 10
BOUNDARIES

Work Friends

Do not bring people in your life who weigh you down. And trust your instincts ... good relationships feel good. They feel right. They don't hurt. They're not painful. That's not just with somebody you want to marry, but it's with the friends that you choose. It's with the people you surround yourselves with.

- Michelle Obama

Do not allow people to occupy unearned and uninvited spaces in your life. You are not required to be friends, trust, or invite your colleagues or co-workers into your personal life or personal spaces. My own mantra when it comes to relationships in the workplace is to keep it business-friendly. It's business, and I'm friendly. However, I am not your friend. I decide who I want to enter into friendships with through informed decision-making based on my interactions and observations of the individual.

KEEP IT BUSINESS-FRIENDLY.

Would you randomly give someone a key to your place of residence? I would hope not. Most likely, a relationship of significance would need to be cultivated before someone was even invited as a guest to your home. Then, a higher level of relationship would be formed for an individual to receive a key to your residence, even as a short-term visitor. For me, the individual would have to be a close family member or friend and demonstrate a high level of good character, trustworthiness, and shared values around cleanliness, noise, boundaries, timeliness, and habits, among other characteristics.

However, when it comes to the workplace, I have seen people jump in headfirst before determining the depth of the water. This is extremely dangerous. I have observed women being harmed because they thought their CEO, supervisor, or co-worker was their friend. Friendship is an agreement between two people. If you make a choice to foster a friendship with someone at work, it should be treated like any other relationship with a few additional layers of accountability because of the dual nature of the blended personal and business relationship.

A paycheck doesn't equal trust or friendship. Just because someone pays you a good salary, allows you a flexible schedule, gives you the office of your dreams, and provides you with the fringe benefits you love doesn't mean they are trustworthy or have your best interest in mind. Your paycheck is payment for the services you provide, a transaction that complies with the employment contract you signed when you were hired. There are legal consequences on various levels for the organization if you are not paid for your work. This may even be your first job or the highest-paying job you have ever had. It's still important to remember that no one is doing you a favor. Your presence and your services benefit the organization as well. The organization is funded and maintains its funding as a result of the work you do. Particularly, it benefits by having you as a team member, especially when you have an extensive career history and your resume, experience, and credentials are submitted in grants and funding requests.

Shared office space, similar roles, or passions don't equate to trust or friendship. We use the word friend way too loosely. We allow people to occupy that space without any prerequisites or accountability. This leaves us vulnerable and sets us up to experience harm. Your paycheck or proximity to your leadership, co-workers, and colleagues should not be an automatic ticket for a front-row seat to your life. You do not owe anyone breakfast, brunch, lunch, dinner, or happy hour. Your personal life is a gift. You should make an informed decision on if and when to share it with others. You decide who you want to share it with and how much you want to share.

Soul Compass

How do you handle personal relationships and friendships at work? What characteristics do you look for in a work friend?

Know Their Story

In recognizing the humanity of our fellow beings, we pay ourselves the highest tribute.

- Thurgood Marshall

During the prior chapters, we discussed assessing and unpacking your bags and suitcases. This is necessary for learning yourself, your story, and how it impacts what enters spaces with you. This influences how you interact with or are triggered by the behaviors and attitudes of others. Now that you have a better understanding of yourself and your story, it's time to learn strategies for understanding the stories of others.

One of the most important aspects of navigating workplace relationships and personalities is knowing a person's story. Their story impacts their beliefs, which, in turn, influences their actions, affecting those around them, including you. Once you are aware, you can develop realistic expectations and proactive response strategies. When we think of boundaries, we often think of them in the physical realm. Boundaries also exist emotionally. I can create a physical boundary and still be significantly impacted because I have not proactively protected my mind. Setting emotional boundaries has been one of the most powerful protective strategies I have implemented in my life and throughout my career.

Life is about balance. When someone's needs or desires are not met in one role of their life, they often overextend or overcompensate to achieve what's lacking through a different role. Think about the various research on the body. When a particular body part is not functioning optimally, other body parts step up to help strengthen the function. For example, if someone has a vision impairment in their left eye, the right eye will naturally go into overdrive to increase their ability to see clearly. If left unaddressed, the capacity of the right eye will begin to diminish over time.

This process occurs emotionally as well. I have found that as adults, we often use adulthood to heal our inner child and childhood, whether consciously or subconsciously. This healing may be from childhood abuse, neglect, bullying, loneliness, fear, or extremely high expectations placed on us by others. Sometimes, the healing is from things and decisions that occurred in adulthood. This healing may be from issues related to marriage, parenting, caregiving, grief, or career and life goals expectations. The challenge often lies in how we overcompensate for a lack in our lives and the processes that we use as a means of healing it. I believe there are three overarching processes.

Process 1

> Do nothing. Maybe the individual doesn't see the problem clearly enough. Maybe they're overwhelmed or feel stuck in the problem. Maybe they're good with the status quo and their ways of being.

Process 2

> The individual uses their power, privileges, influence, and role to heal their inner child and adult. Maybe the individual felt alone as a child. As a leader, they engage in behaviors that keep people close to them, such as micromanaging their staff or engaging in inappropriate boundaries. The staff that comply are looked upon favorable and incentivized. Those who are resistant are penalized.

Process 3

> The individual does their inner work through self-reflection, therapy, self-help tools (books, podcasts, activities), forgiveness, mentorship, coaching, prayer, meditation, an accountability buddy, healing spaces, or implementing other positive healing strategies.

> Remember, each of us brings something to the office from our personal lives because we are human. How we heal influences how we show up. Imagine what this looks like at the office. Think of your most challenging relationships and apply this lens. Here is a scenario to walk through.

The Story of Leader A

Leader A grew up feeling like she always had to prove herself to those around her. Her siblings made the honor roll throughout their primary school years, and she always struggled to pass her classes. Her siblings received praise from her parents, and her parents pushed her to do better and bring home good grades like her siblings. After graduating high school, Leader A decided she had enough of school. Her siblings went on to pursue their post-secondary education and achieved advanced degrees. Leader A's family gatherings now consist of her siblings talking about their homes, cars, careers, income, dreams, and luxury aspirations. After working 15 years at the same company, Leader A was promoted to department manager.

How will Leader A show up in this new role? Let's use the options listed above. This is not the gospel, meaning these things might not necessarily play out in this manner. These examples support you in developing mindset models and healthy boundaries when working with others.

Process 1 In Action

> Leader A comes in oozing. She wants to be valued and complimented because there is a lack of these things currently in her life. As a result, she engages in people-pleasing behaviors. She is nice, flexible, and maintains good relationships with her staff. On the contrary, she experiences challenges when it comes to making uncomfortable decisions or advocating for staff to upper management.

Process 2 In Action

> Leader A comes in with a chip on her shoulders. She is frustrated because it has taken so long for her to be promoted to management. In contrast, her siblings and

others in the organization seem to climb the career ladder effortlessly. She has also developed an attitude that she will do whatever it takes to maintain her position and promote higher within the organization. Leader A is overbearing and rigid and micromanages her staff.

Process 3 In Action

Leader A enters her role as someone striving to heal. She is not intimidated by her siblings' achievements and is not in competition with anyone else. Leader A desires to create her own path by being the leader she desires to follow. She is flexible, intentional, authentic, and cares about the success of the staff and the organization.

Again, these are just examples of how Leader A could show up at the office. This scenario contains a minimal number of intersections. Additional intersecting identities and characteristics could significantly change the outcomes of each process. These intersections include race, gender, marital/relationship health, parenting health, physical health factors, degree, lived experiences, and more.

What should you do if you don't know a person's story? You could be intentional and sincere about cultivating an authentic relationship. Remember, a personal or beyond-business relationship is an agreement between two parties. The other person has the right not to enter a beyond-business relationship with you. Respect that. You also have the right not to be in a beyond-business relationship with others. Without a beyond-business relationship, you could create a private story through a lens of love, care, empathy, and compassion. This is a story you develop (and keep private) about the person to understand better and have grace for them despite their behaviors. I have created many private stories over the years. Over time, I have found the private stories I created to be true about 95% of the time.

Why is the story of others important? Because most people are often trying to heal their inner child or adult. The story is a protective strategy for you as a person who is interacting with them. It decreases the chances of you making the behavior of others about you or taking it personally. Taking it personally, when it is not personal, has a significant impact on our well-being. My guiding rule is that if someone is a jerk to me and cordial to everyone else, that's personal and requires a conversation. If someone is a jerk to me and everyone else, that's on them, not me. It doesn't mean that I am impacted less by their behavior. However, it does change how I respond to their behavior. I can respond differently because it's not specifically about me. I enter the spaces I share with them, expecting them to behave in a certain way. This way, I am not ambushed or caught off guard. I'm surprised, not broken, if they don't behave as expected.

Grace and Accountability

Being held accountable is an act of generosity and compassion. It is a gift that someone gives us to correct our wrongs, unlearn, and do better for the sake of our own growth. It might be uncomfortable, but it is worth the discomfort.

- Minaa B

Understanding the stories of others is critical to seeing the humanity of others. It is key to developing strategies to interact with individuals in a way that leaves their dignity intact and simultaneously protects your humanity and well-being.

That kind of grace is amazing. Grace is sweet. It is not a pass to abuse or mistreat others repeatedly. It is also not a pass to allow yourself to be abused or mistreated. However, I have seen and experienced grace being abused on numerous occasions. I have experienced leaders who have no intentions of improving themselves using grace as a manipulation tool. Just like all things in the world, people with poor intentions will find ways to capitalize on the vulnerabilities of others.

Grace and Christianity are two things that I have experienced and observed being exploited in the workplace. I found myself being victimized by this early on in my career. It eventually forced me to take a step back, pull up, and realize what was occurring. Do not allow anyone to use grace and Christianity as leverage to use and abuse you. What would Jesus do? Jesus would not want you to be abused, exploited, or manipulated.

Grace is a compound that requires accountability to be effective in any successful relationship, including the workplace. Grace is unearned favor and forgiveness. Accountability is proactively taking responsibility for one's actions. I call this the peanut butter and jelly sandwich. Accountability is the peanut butter, and grace is the jelly. The bread represents the relationship between two people. Everyone loves jelly—it's sweet and smooth. The peanut butter, though, can be a force to be reckoned with, especially if it's extra crunchy. It sticks to the roof of your mouth and gums and requires work to process and fully digest. However, all three items are needed to make the sandwich.

GRACE IS A COMPOUND THAT REQUIRES ACCOUNTABILITY TO BE EFFECTIVE IN ANY SUCCESSFUL RELATIONSHIP, INCLUDING THE WORKPLACE.

The absence of grace results in condemning individuals for making human mistakes. The lack of accountability gives individuals a pass not to be their best selves, not to do their self-work, and provides a green light to continue making the same (or similar) mistakes repeatedly and not take action to rectify how they show up. It's similar to someone stepping on your toes and apologizing, stepping on your toes again and apologizing, and then repeating the cycle over and over. At some point, their actions and the impact of them continuously ignoring the pain they are causing you will create an imbalance that far exceeds the gift of your grace. Their apologies eventually become null.

Grace should not be a one-directional expectation, nor should it be given out in that manner. This is extremely dangerous and destructive, and it's rooted in colonization and privilege abuse. Accountability is the work that builds muscle. Muscles are necessary to lean into and engage in difficult but necessary conversations on race, equity, justice, access, anti-racism, and shared power in a healthy and productive manner. Muscles are essential to stand firm in the face of discomfort and resist the deep urges to avoid, divert, gaslight, racelight, retaliate, or double down on wrongs. As the muscles grow, so does stamina to reflect versus react, take action versus do nothing, and stand up versus blend in.

Soul Compass

What do grace and accountability mean to you? How do they show up in your expectations for yourself and others?

CHAPTER 11
SELF-PRESERVATION & RECLAMATION

Forgiveness Is Freedom

For me, forgiveness and compassion are always linked: how do we hold people accountable for wrongdoing and yet at the same time remain in touch with their humanity enough to believe in their capacity to be transformed?

- bell hooks

Forgiveness is the key to your freedom. You must find the space to forgive yourself and others. Unforgiveness is like a funky vacation swimsuit collection. It started out fresh and cute. It became funky over time because it was slightly wet from being in the water. You hung it over your balcony, but it didn't dry completely, so you temporarily placed it in a plastic bag until you got home. However, when you got home, you didn't remove it. It has now been in your suitcase since you returned home from vacation, and weeks have passed.

To make matters worse, you went on more vacations and added more swimsuits that have become funky. No matter how many clean and cute outfits you pack, they will all be funky because they share a suitcase with the funky swimsuit collection. Eventually, there will be no room for clean and cute outfits or souvenirs for yourself and others because the funky swimsuits will consume the suitcase.

In a previous chapter, we discussed the suitcase, which represents the things we carry with us throughout our lives. Everyone has a suitcase. The swimsuits represent our life experiences, good, bad, and ugly. The water represents the Rough S.E.A.S. —Soul Eroding Assimilation-Forcing Systems we have navigated. Unforgiveness is the mildew and funk build-up on the swimsuits and adjacent items over time when the swimsuits are not dried, laundered, and cared for properly. This is how unforgiveness affects us and everything we do. We become so overwhelmed by unforgiveness and adjacent emotions—such as resentment, anger, fear, skewed perceptions of self, helplessness, hopelessness, and paranoia—that our innovation and purpose are diminished.

Forgiveness cultivates a path for reconciliation, restoration, and healing. Reconciliation and healing enable us to take those funky swimsuits out of our suitcases and inspect them. Some swimsuits can be restored through cleaning. Some are non-restorable and will need to be discarded. Some have been in our suitcase for quite some time. They can be restored, but we have outgrown them. Once we have reconciled our suitcases, we make room for our restored swimsuits and new ones. We also make space for our cute outfits (self-care, self-love) and souvenirs (gifts for us and others).

FORGIVENESS CULTIVATES A PATH FOR RECONCILIATION, RESTORATION, AND HEALING.

Forgiveness as a Leader

There's a great chance that if you have been in a leadership role, you have unintentionally contributed to harming others. There's a great chance you have remained silent amid harm being done to others out of fear or exhaustion. There's also a great chance that you have advocated for better treatment for others, and your voice was unheard, or your advocacy was met with inaction or retaliation. It may have appeared to others that you were not doing anything, not doing enough, or worse, that you had fallen in alignment with the individuals causing harm. You might have even felt and thought these things about yourself.

I have been in formal leadership roles for the majority of my career, so I am not exempt from this. I have come to terms with the harms I contributed to, those I didn't use my voice or power to advocate for, and the numerous times I advocated behind the scenes and loudly to no avail or to my own detriment. I had to reflect and take inventory of my experiences. I had to make amends internally and commit to being more aware of myself and how I show up. I had to create a plan and move forward. I now check in with those that I lead to assess my impact. I aim to minimize the harm I unintentionally cause and contribute to.

Most likely, if you're reading this book, you are striving to learn, be, and do better each day. That's admirable! Breathe and give yourself grace and love for that. It's easy to get caught up in being promoted and lose sight of how you may be being exploited or used as a pawn to contribute to the harm or oppression of others. This is not a pass or excuse but an acknowledgment of possible origins and contributors. Life is about choices, and we must know the "why" of our choices and decisions. There is power and healing in truths. Forgive yourself for the times and occasions when you could have been a better leader. The silver lining is that you are alive and breathing. Your breath means you have options and opportunities to make new decisions and choices right now, in this very moment. You can choose to be different than you were last year, yesterday, or earlier today.

Forgiveness for Those Who Have Harmed You

Forgive others. Forgive those who have harmed you. Carrying unforgiveness will destroy you and make you unwell. Imagine a pipe where water can flow smoothly and unrestricted. Now imagine your body as that pipe and the water as your authentic gifts, innovative thoughts, joy, wellness, bright light, positive energy, and all the things you are and were created to be. Unforgiveness is pipe gunk. It's the nasty residue and grease that causes blockages. If we are not careful, unforgiveness will result in a suboptimal flow or complete blockage of our divine gifts. Nothing can enter or exit. It will impact our ability to influence our communities and the world positively. If we allow the pipe gunk to build up without any interventions, it will cause not only a blockage but also a backup. A backup that will spill over on others. It will ultimately overwhelm, sting, burn, and hurt those who genuinely love us and those we were called to help, support, or be in a community with.

No living person is immune to pipe gunk. Life can be challenging, and human beings can be a force to be reckoned with daily. Our interactions with others will undoubtedly contribute to our pipe gunk. The goal is to increase awareness of its presence and impact and proactively be prepared to degunk our pipes expeditiously and daily. What is degunking? Letting go of harmful thoughts. Refraining from self-destructive behaviors. Letting go of emotions, even those justifiable if they do not serve us well. We must be wiser in our decisions to interact with individuals whose behaviors trigger negative emotions and immerse ourselves in things that support us in breathing and pressing reset. We must surround ourselves with people who support us, make our hearts smile, and ignite our joy lamps.

Soul Compass

What does forgiveness look like for you? Is this something you struggle with? What actions can you take to improve?

Reclaim Your Joy

Black joy is the heartbeat and pulse of our survival, our resiliency, our perseverance, our health and wellbeing.

- Anita Dashiell-Sparks

Some things are non-negotiable. Some things can't be bought, sold, or taken unless we allow it. And our joy is one of these things. In the words of one of my favorite songs from church, *the world didn't give it, and the world can't take it away*. Our joy is our unique and divine gift from our Creator. I like to think of joy as our lifelong umbilical cord to our Creator. It's how we receive deposits of the supernatural and intangible things necessary to navigate and thrive. It complements our faith. It's an active emotion that's difficult to describe, yet one of the most powerful forces that we possess.

However, if we don't fully understand its purpose and power, it's easy to allow our joy to be stolen. Stolen in the challenges and struggles that we endure. The ones that make us feel alone and suck at our desire to press forward. The challenges and struggles that make us sometimes question if there is a higher power at work or if people are just allowed to cause harm without any consequences.

If we really knew the purpose and power of our joy, we would protect and nurture it by all means. Our joy is essentially our lifeline. We cannot afford to lose it or have it eroded. Without joy, our life lacks clarity of purpose, hopefulness, peace, perseverance, prosperity, and more. This impacts our power, confidence, fierceness, and wellness.

Sometimes, we conflate joy with happiness; they are not the same. Happiness is situational and dependent on our emotions (feelings, thoughts, mood, energy), external circumstances (interactions with people and systems), and our environment (physical or virtual location). It varies. Happiness is important, but it is also superficial.

Joy is a constant internal light that is not dependent on anything else to do what it was created to do. Joy is the feeling that we get in our bodies and bones that reminds us that there is something at work that's bigger than us or our thoughts. It's the smile through the tears, knowing things will be okay regardless of the situation. It's the feeling of purpose and knowing that our life is bigger than our current circumstances. Joy is the indescribable feeling of, *"Woman, you haven't seen anything yet. Don't believe me? Just watch."* It's unconditional and divine hope, help, and support. Joy ignites the mindset necessary to keep going, the courage to become unstuck, and the power to move mountains. Joy is key to our freedom!

JOY IGNITES THE MINDSET NECESSARY TO KEEP GOING, THE COURAGE TO BECOME UNSTUCK, AND THE POWER TO MOVE MOUNTAINS.

Here are some examples of activities to reclaim your joy:

- Engage in at least one small activity that makes your heart smile on a daily basis. If you are just starting this journey, you can start with a weekly goal and then incrementally increase it to a daily goal. You can even add the activities to a joy journal or take photos and create a digital joy log.

- Therapy works. Find a great therapist that specializes in working with people like you. You can narrow your focus by race, ethnicity, gender, issue, and the support level you seek. Once you find a great match, follow through and be consistent.

- Limit your exposure to negative messaging and bad news. I am intentional about when and what news and other media I expose myself to. I even have the start-up and new tab screens on my computer set to a good news home page.

- Exercise gratitude. Practice being grateful for what you have each day. Start from your feet and work upward to your head (i.e., mobility, mental wellness, use of limbs, independence). Then, move to the things around you (i.e., clean water, hot water, a roof over your head). Then, to your supporters, friends, family, and other loved ones.

- Create a joy playlist. I am a fan of creating playlists on my phone. This enables me to take my theme music wherever I go. Create a playlist of songs that bring you joy and bring up happy memories, thoughts, and dreams.

- Find a community. Find or engage in activities you love or a new hobby with others. Zumba is my go-to. I also enjoy pickleball, educational programs, and concerts.

Soul Compass

What people, places, or things ignite your joy? How are you protecting and nurturing your joy?

Reclaim Your Wellness

The goal is to grow so strong on the inside that nothing on the outside can affect your inner wellness without your conscious permission.

- Author Unknown

Have you ever seen an award for the most burned-out and dead employee of the year? There's no reward for overworking until you are unwell, disabled, or deceased. I've had the unfortunate experience of knowing multiple people who believed they would grind now and rest later. The sad part of the story is that some of them are now deceased or disabled. They were never able to enjoy the fruits of their harvest. There's only one you. There's something in between living and dying: suffering. Sometimes, life throws us curve balls that result in suffering. Sometimes, suffering results from the cumulative neglect to care for an issue, problem, or condition. Please do not choose to suffer by neglecting your health and wellness. There is only one you, and you only have one body and one mind. Be diligent in taking care of yourself.

I have seen so many women, Black women including myself, who put their health and well-being on the back burner. For some, it's not on a burner at all. It's completely neglected. What is internal will manifest itself externally. What occurs externally will manifest itself internally. If we expect to achieve our mission, purpose, and goals, we must nourish our mind, body, and soul. This must become a priority we intentionally make time for and not an optional task that we will get around to. It's using our vacation days, sick days, personal holidays, and other time allowances to care for ourselves and not wearing unused and rollover hours as a badge of honor. One of my favorite sayings from my mom is, "I have never seen a U-Haul with a person's belongings at the cemetery. We can't take nothing with us when we die."

Developing financial goals and creating a legacy for our children and loved ones is beautiful and something we should all aspire towards. However, we cannot build these things effectively if we are ill or incapacitated. We must develop a self-care plan for our mind, body, and soul. It is even more critical that we follow through and take action to implement it daily. I block out personal time on my calendar and create reminders for myself. Initially, you can start small, taking five or ten minutes each day for yourself and spending time doing something you enjoy. It doesn't require buying anything or going anywhere unless you choose to. You can choose to sit quietly. Doing nothing is doing something. You will be surprised how a little time can make a big difference. Wellness is freedom.

Here are some examples of activities to reclaim your wellness:

Mind

Read, watch, engage with, or listen to things that replenish and renew your mind. Things that get your brain juices going. Examples include reading or listening to the Bible or spiritual service; listening to a podcast that expands your current learning and thinking or creates new channels; watching cartoons, comedy, or something that ignites your inner child; engaging in conversation with individuals who seek to grow, learn, and improve themselves; prayer and meditation; engaging in counseling, therapy, and coaching; honoring your commitment to take your mental wellness medications as prescribed.

Body

Get preventive, regular medical and wellness checks based on your age, gender, medical history, and genetics. Honor any commitments made to taking wellness and preventative medications as prescribed. Monitor your health and seek medical treatment as soon as possible for abnormalities and differences. Pursue dental care and cleanings. Spend time with yourself and your body, noting changes and conducting recommended breast and other self-exams. Exercise regularly with stretching, yoga, pickleball, dance, swimming, walking, jogging, Zumba, and more.

Soul

Nurturing your soul involves engaging in activities that bring joy, peace, and fulfillment. It can include any of the actions listed above. It can also include volunteering with local organizations or events, practicing prayer or spiritual gratitude, attending retreats or creating your own zen space/moment, being in a community with friends and loved ones who pour into you, and traveling to new or familiar places that bring you joy and peace.

Wellness and self-preservation in the workplace look different for each individual. Some women fight, some leave the organization, some retreat, some compartmentalize their experiences, and others soothe the offenders through people-pleasing behaviors. Whatever path you choose, it should be paved with healthy actions and should position you to unlock the fullest potential of your power, wellness, and joy. Life is not promised to any of us; it is a precious gift. We are not owed the blessing of living to see retirement, see next year, next month, tomorrow, or even our next breath. This is why it's so vital for us to live now. Live life to the fullest and enjoy it responsibly. Bills and debt are here to stay. They have been an aspect of human life for centuries and will be here forever, even after we leave this Earth. Life should be measured in quality over quantity. Ultimately, I would love to live a long, healthy life filled with achieving my dreams, watching loved ones achieve their dreams, and creating fond memories. I want this for you as well. This is the legacy that exceeds time, money, and circumstances.

LIFE IS NOT PROMISED TO ANY OF US;
IT IS A PRECIOUS GIFT.

Soul Compass

What does wellness mean to you? What actions are you taking to reclaim your wellness?

Reclaim Your Power

The most common way people give up their power is by thinking they don't have any.

- **Alice Walker**

We don't jump out of the water because of the waves. We turn our fear into fierceness. We become stronger despite the waves. We enhance our skills to predict wave patterns and use our unique tools to manage them. We become navigators.

WE DON'T JUMP OUT OF THE WATER BECAUSE OF THE WAVES. WE TURN OUR FEAR INTO FIERCENESS.

As long as there is breath in our bodies, there will always be waves to navigate. We can develop a mindset that generalizes all water as dangerous waves because of the Rough S.E.A.S. we are currently navigating or have experienced. This will prevent us from fully enjoying all of the other wonderful things the water could bring us and lead us to. Imagine being so afraid of water that you refused to go to the beach, go on a cruise, or fly in a plane that will travel across the ocean. You would essentially be landlocked and lose out on the opportunity to visit several states and countries, be in a community with diverse individuals, and immerse yourself in a plethora of beautiful cultures. You owe it to yourself to address the underlying things preventing you from living and experiencing your best life.

Toxic and abusive organizations will continue to exist as long as people continue to participate in harmful and oppressive behaviors. However, we don't have to continue to be the victims. We can do our part to protect ourselves by taking proactive steps to recognize it earlier and put measures in place to repel or buffer the impacts. The goal is to live in our authenticity despite the waves. To navigate the world with the power and joy we were gifted before birth. The goal is achieving maximum mental, physical, social, emotional, and spiritual wellness. Power is freedom.

Here are some examples of activities to reclaim your power:

- Identify your personal and career aspirations, and develop small achievable goals and action steps that you can take to achieve them. Celebrate your accomplishments.

- Sharpen your skills. Find something you are passionate about and immerse yourself in learning about it and becoming an expert in it.

- Develop an inspiration board or affirmation wall. Find quotes from individuals who you look up to and surround yourself with them. I have quotes and affirmations on sticky notes on my computer monitor, the walls in my office, and my vehicle. I previously had one on my bathroom mirror.

- Master the art of saying NO without feeling guilty. So much of our power is given to others. We yield to the thoughts and feelings of others before taking care of ourselves. Saying no is healthy, and it's great for creating healthy boundaries.

- Say something positive about yourself on a daily basis. On the days you struggle to think of something, thank yourself for making it through the day.

- Develop a personal power profile. This is a list of things that you love about yourself. Strive to add new things on at least a monthly basis.

- Give yourself grace when you make mistakes. Learn from your mistakes and use the lessons learned to enhance yourself and those around you.

- Celebrate your accomplishments and wins—all of them. Some of us are so great at celebrating others but not so great when it comes to celebrating ourselves. Take time to celebrate your small and big achievements.

Soul Compass

What does it mean to reclaim your power? What difference does your power make?

Find Your Community

Anything is possible when you have the right people there to support you.

- Misty Copeland

A few years ago, my husband and I went on a cruise. During the cruise, there was an amazing nighttime water acrobatic show. The show was phenomenal! The acrobatic team took a short break during the show and then returned. The next morning, my husband and I turned on the television to the cruise path channel, noticed the ship had taken a slightly altered path, and then returned to the charted path. We were curious as to what occurred and made many guesses. Later that day, we had an opportunity to attend a meet and greet with the captain. We asked him about the altered course. He told us that his team of shipmates told him about the winds during the water acrobatic show and requested permission to slightly alter the route to prevent canceling the show. He approved. The ship's path was then slightly altered, the show continued, and afterward, the ship returned to the previously charted path. I found this to be so fascinating. The fact that the show was able to continue without a significant pause. The fact that the captain's shipmates had the foresight to create an altered route to present for his approval. The fact that the captain trusted his shipmates to make solid decisions in his absence to navigate the ship as he would or better.

This taught me a valuable lesson: while each of us is the captain of our ship, every captain needs a team of navigators and shipmates to support them. An individual or group of individuals to help you navigate your journey. People who are willing to stand and take action on what you deeply care about even when they don't fully understand. People who will hold you accountable to being the best version of yourself even when the truth will hurt your feelings because they care about you and want to see you win and thrive.

The goal of the virus that keeps virusing is to make us paranoid and fearful of being hurt by one another. This keeps us apart. We are stronger together, and we can make change together. We must be open to opportunities to be in a community with others. Every captain needs shipmates they can trust with decisions and their life. Every woman deserves to have a place where everyone knows her name. A place where people look forward to her coming. A place where she is missed when she's not there. A Black Cheers or a Nipsey's Bar and Restaurant.

> EVERY WOMAN DESERVES TO HAVE A PLACE WHERE EVERYONE KNOWS HER NAME. A PLACE WHERE PEOPLE LOOK FORWARD TO HER COMING.

It's not too late.

Within every group, there is a person or a few people that we just naturally click with. This presents opportunities to cultivate a friendship. I am always in awe when I hear people talk about strong friendships they have cultivated since elementary or middle school. I felt that my time for this level of friendship had passed since I could not rewind my life to childhood. Here's what I learned. God is the Father of time. HE can fast-forward relationships and bonds. It's nothing for Him to allow our paths to cross with individuals we meet in a moment and feel like we've known them all our lives. We just have to desire it and invite these opportunities.

I know this to be true because I prayed and asked God to help me to be a great friend who attracts great friends. Let me tell you something: God did that for me, and HE can do it for you too! You never know—that woman in the grocery line, sitting at the next table in the restaurant, in Zumba class, sitting on the airplane next to you, in your training or conference, or providing you with a service at your favorite spot could be your next best buddy.

Soul Compass

Are you open to meeting and fostering healthy relationships with Black women? Are you open to meeting and fostering healthy relationships with diverse people different from you? What actions can you take to enhance these opportunities?

What About Your Friends

*Surround yourself with only people
who are going to lift you higher.*

- Oprah Winfrey

In the early 90s, the music group TLC had a popular song, *What About Your Friends*. The song refers to friends as people who have your back through thick and thin, who accept you, and who stand their ground when it comes to the relationship. This means different things to different people. The gist is that your inner circle matters. Who you are friends with matters.

YOUR INNER CIRCLE MATTERS.

In a previous chapter, I discussed the dangers of haphazardly using the term "friend" without boundaries, standards, or accountability. I believe friendships are mutually beneficial agreements between two or more people. Friendships require mutual accountability, reciprocity, grace, forgiveness, love, flexibility, and more. These are just a few foundational things. You should also intentionally add things specific to your preferences (likes/dislikes), needs, and the season in life you are in and striving towards. We also need to circle back on our long-time friendships to examine their impact on our lives. Sometimes, we hold on to people because we have known them since we were little, since college, since our last favorite job, or since we lived in (fill in the blank) state/city/country. As I navigate the journey of maturity and evolution, I have learned and am still learning things about myself and my friendships. Here are a few.

1. A friend can be someone you don't speak to daily. Of course, you want to check in with one another regularly, but this may not be daily or weekly. However, you are there for one another in times of need.

2. We have to be open to the fact that some of our friendships will be lifelong, and some will be term-limited. I have been guilty of holding on past an expiration date on more than one occasion. It has been disastrous and led to unnecessary pain. This is life, and people outgrow relationships. To be

successful in this area, we must master the art of saying farewell and closing chapters.

3. If I am unaware of my needs and the direction I am heading, it will be hard for me to assess my friendships effectively. I must do my self-work first to better understand my needs, desires, and deal breakers.

4. We must be intentional about the structure on which we build relationships. If we build them on a strong foundation, they will last throughout their intended season. If we build relationships on quicksand, they will dissolve just as fast as they were created. If we build the relationship on a strong foundation but never check back, we may be surprised to learn that it has developed cracks over time, just like a house with a settling foundation. Strong winds and storms will come. The foundation determines what the relationship can withstand over time.

5. There are friends, and there are riders. I believe riders are those next-level friends. The friends that roll up their sleeves and pitch in before you ask for help. They are the ones who know you so well that they sense your energy and know when something is not going right for you. They are the ones that all they need is who, what, and where, and they are there to support you. I am grateful for the riders in my life and feel blessed to reciprocate.

Your friends and inner circle should help and support you in winning in life, period. These close relationships should be based on reciprocity, which does not equate to an act for an act or a gift for a gift. The reciprocity should be based on each individual's capacity, skills, and talents, and it is oftentimes non-monetary. People will have ups and downs and enter and exit various seasons throughout their lifetimes. So, their capacity to support you may vary, and vice versa. Along the way, conversations are critical to clarify misunderstandings and assumptions.

On the other hand, sometimes life changes people and causes them to regress in their goals, values, and roles. As a result, they may lose their capacity to support you in a healthy way. This could be detrimental to your present and future, so you must be willing to move quickly. For this reason, it is extremely important to take note of the changes and reevaluate your friendship on a consistent basis. You always want to surround yourself with people who will support and celebrate your soaring.

Soul Compass

What are your requirements for cultivating a friendship with someone? What are your deal breakers? Who are your riders?

CHAPTER 12
THE INTERSECTION OF WHAT NEXT?

What's In It For Me

It is so liberating to really know what I want, what truly makes me happy, what I will not tolerate. I have learned that it is no one else's job to take care of me but me.

- **Beyonce Knowles-Carter**

If you have ever flown, you may be aware of the flight attendant's safety announcement before departure. During this announcement, the flight attendant urges passengers, in the event of an emergency, to take care of themselves first. Passengers are informed that oxygen masks will drop from overhead if there is a sudden loss of cabin pressure. Passengers are urged to put on their oxygen masks before assisting their children and other passengers. Why are passengers instructed to take care of themselves first? Could it be that the only way we can support others in living is by first living ourselves? What would it look and feel like to take care of yourself first? Would it be an uncomfortable or common practice?

Warning: this may be triggering. I am requesting that you pause and put on your selfish hat for a moment. For many Black women, this feels wrong. We have been nurtured, socialized, acculturated, and indoctrinated to care for others first and to place the needs of others before our own. We have been shamed and made to feel bad or less than optimal in our roles as employees, parents, caregivers, family members, and friends for even thinking of prioritizing ourselves. Deep and meaningful self-care requires us to be selfish. It requires us to pause the tape on everyone else's needs, wants, desires, and demands of us and prioritize our own needs, wants, desires, and demands. How does prioritizing yourself look, sound, and feel in your personal life?

Prioritizing ourselves should not be isolated to our personal lives. It should also transfer to the workplace. We spend a significant amount of our waking hours at work, so if we compartmentalize and limit our prioritization to our personal lives, we will limit our ability to thrive and maximize our wellness. Prioritizing yourself at work can look various ways, depending on your preferences, personality, and work environments. Here are some examples.

- Take all of your breaks: Most companies, at minimum, allow for two 15-minute breaks and a 30 or 60-minute lunch break. Get in the habit of taking all of your breaks. Get out of the office when possible, even if it means sitting in your vehicle or taking a short walk. If these are not viable options, stay in your office but silence your computer and work phone. Find something exciting to engage in. Short YouTube videos, puzzles (app or live), texting or calling a friend or family member, or engaging in an adult coloring book.

- Pursue professional development opportunities: What are your goals and interests? Are there any training, webinars, conferences, or meet-up opportunities you can participate in? I have seen women become so comfortable in their work roles that they stop learning, growing, and evolving. This contributes to the notion of being stuck in a role and circumstance. Your development should be a priority. Development can come in many forms: courses, certifications, communities of practice, affinity groups, and more. These activities often serve as keys to networking with diverse individuals, building skills, shifting mindsets, and receiving encouragement. Most organizations have budgets to support these opportunities. If not, and the fee is feasible, you can pay it yourself. There may be some tax deductions available to you.

- Saying NO: No is a complete sentence. Do not overload yourself mentally or physically by accepting or taking on additional tasks that result in you being exhausted, overwhelmed, and overworked to the point where you cannot effectively care for yourself. Work was here before we were born and will be here after we leave this Earth. Yes, there are seasons when our work peaks, but it should be short and deliverable, like reports or grant submissions in nature, and not a weekly occurrence. If you burn out or become ill, the company will figure out how to get the work done. More than likely, the work you are sacrificing yourself to complete would be divided and given to two or three staff members. The response you receive from your leadership when you say no indicates the organization's culture. Don't take it personally.

- Use your vacation and personal time. You can plan a trip and go away or enjoy a staycation at home, watching movies in your pajamas. You decide what you want to do and how you want to spend your time. Be sure to unplug completely from work. No checking or responding to work emails, texts, intra-agency message boards, or phone calls. No reading or writing grants, catching up on reports, or conducting employee annual reviews. Repeat after me: NO work-related stuff will be performed or facilitated while I am out of the office. If your team cannot navigate their roles or make decisions while you are out of the office for a few days, bigger leadership issues are at play.

No life or honorary achievement awards exist for the person with the most unused vacation time. There are no life awards for the person who was most available while they were out on vacation or sick leave. If your organization is engaging in this type of celebration, it is cultivating and reinforcing a toxic and dehumanizing culture that prioritizes productivity over people. This needs to be discontinued immediately. Taking breaks from and during work is critical and healthy.

Additionally, I have not observed many people who fare well from overworking themselves. In fact, it's often the opposite. They are unwell and unhealthy. Remember, there is a place between living and dying; it's called suffering. Don't choose to suffer by neglecting yourself. Choose to prioritize YOU!

Soul Compass

In prioritizing yourself at work, how does this look, sound, and feel? What are you doing for yourself? What opportunities align with your goals and are available to you?

Preparing for the Pivot

I have discovered in life that there are ways of getting almost anywhere you want to go if you really want to go.

- Langston Hughes

If we believe in the power of the Creator that allowed us to be and sustained us in our current role, why wouldn't that same Creator assist us in finding another role within our organization or another organization and sustain us there as well? In addition to that, we could obtain favor, a great salary and benefits, and support from an amazing team of colleagues. If we have made magic in our current circumstances, then we have the power, skills, and abilities to make that magic happen elsewhere, too. Pivoting requires us to get out of our fear brain and think with our fierceness brain. Otherwise, we become stuck. Trapped in and by our minds.

In many instances, "stuck" is a mindset. It's the intersection of knowing what must be done but not having the confidence, skills, knowledge, or resources to make it happen. It can also be the intersection of identifying the situation as something in which we have given our all and not knowing what to do next. Often, what keeps us stuck is the thought that there's something more we can do at the organization we are currently employed by and the thought that we may be giving up too soon. It's the fear of missing out on opportunities on either side of the situation. The unanswered questions are: How long should I stay and deal with this abuse? What if it doesn't work out in the next organization? "Stuck" is lacking a viable next option or opportunity.

Things may need to be done and said at your organization. However, there may be nothing left for you to do or say. Sometimes, you are not the messenger or person to lead that change. Maybe you have code-switched, nipped and folded, tucked and rolled, and shrunk yourself into miniature versions that are less threatening or more comforting, and it's still not good enough. There's no one else you can be or morph into. Maybe you have lost more than you have gained emotionally. You have given more than you have received, and in many ways, you are emotionally bankrupt. It doesn't mean your time, work, and energy were in vain. It means your purpose in this season at that organization was to till the soil and plant the seeds for change. It may be someone else's season to water, fertilize, and care for the harvest. Maybe it's time to evolve beyond what you see in front of you. This starts with your mindset.

There must always be an emotional pivot before a physical pivot. It helps ground your mind, heart, feelings, and thoughts. Pivots enable us to be proactive and responsive versus reactive and impulsive. Pivoting does not mean you are giving up or that you are soft. Pivoting is a power move. It is the reclamation of your power, wellness, and joy. It's your intentional reset and recalibration to your purpose and the person you were created to be so that you can do the things you were created to do. This increases the probability of your success.

PIVOTING IS A POWER MOVE.

Soul Compass

Are you prepared to pivot? What does your pivot look like?

Enter With an Exit Plan

Every great dream begins with a dreamer. Always remember, you have within you the strength, the patience, and the passion to reach for the stars to change the world.

— Harriet Tubman

I am a fan of plans. I love a good plan of action! The project manager in me geeks out on plans. So, it's natural for me to use plans in various areas of my life to help me become unstuck. Here's a personal example. I used to experience a delay in my response to crises. If something occurred in my presence, I would freeze for several seconds before responding. One day, during an annual workplace CPR training, the fireman instructor shared an observation to help me navigate this situation. He said, "You are very analytical, so you freeze before responding because your brain pauses to analyze the situation step-by-step." He then proceeded to provide me with a tip that I use to this day. "To better navigate situations, prepare yourself by thinking of potential scenarios ahead of time. Think about what could potentially happen in a given space or situation and prepare a response. Then, if something happens, you are ready to respond quickly." Implementing that tip changed my mindset about entering spaces and significantly improved my response time.

Here's another example of a plan in action. I previously worked at an organization that took risk management extremely seriously and did a great job in facilitating responses to various risks. Not only was there a detailed emergency plan in place, but there were scheduled drills and simulations. During the drills, an emergency situation would be simulated with participation from all employees in the building on that day, and announcements would be sent to those working elsewhere. The processes were comprehensive, easy to understand, and well-organized. There were two primary goals for developing and implementing the plans. First, to ensure everyone is informed and prepared in an emergency. Second, to identify successes, challenges, and areas for improvement with the plan. If an actual emergency occurred, staff would be equipped with the proper resources and prepared to respond quickly.

What if we entered the workplace with this strategy in mind? Entering with a viable action plan. With a plan of action in the case of an emergency or crisis. An emergency or crisis that required us to protect and reclaim our power, wellness, and joy. How powerful would it be, physically and emotionally, if we entered the workplace with a plan of action? Based on the data shared previously in the prevalence report chapter, we know that as Black women, if we are not already Navigating Rough S.E.A.S. —Soul Eroding Assimilation-Forcing Systems, it may be a matter of time before we face them. Therefore, it would be proactive to have a plan in place. I have found that sometimes people get nervous when I mention having a plan of action in place. It makes them feel like they are being secretive, cheating on the organization, or not giving their work their all. Let's dispel these myths now.

HOW POWERFUL WOULD IT BE, PHYSICALLY AND EMOTIONALLY, IF WE ENTERED THE WORKPLACE WITH A PLAN OF ACTION?

Being secretive. Since when does the organization need to know everything about us and our lives? I would bet that we don't tell our organizational leaders everything anyway. That would not be wise. Surprise, they don't tell us everything either. Did you receive a call from your CEO this morning informing you what color and type of clothing they were thinking about wearing? Or what they really think about some of their employees and board members? Most likely not. Hopefully, that individual demonstrates discernment and boundaries regarding what they share with staff. If this helps, instead of being secretive, think of it as protecting your innovative brainstorming sessions until you are ready to actualize them.

Cheating on the organization. For some individuals, even the thought of being open to other opportunities feels like cheating. My question is, where does this sentiment stem from? Where did you learn to feel this way about prioritizing yourself? Does it have ties to colonization? Respectfully, does your organization's leadership have the same level of loyalty and love for you?

Would you commit to marrying someone who abused you in hopes that one day they would magically change? Change requires a desire to take the necessary actions to be a better human being. Is your organization's leadership actively taking steps toward positive change? Remember, change should be progressive and have visible receipts.

Here's another question that comes to mind for me in terms of reciprocity. If your organization were struggling financially and planning to close its doors, how much notice would they give you? Please do not conflate this with how much notice you want to receive. Would they provide you with severance pay? A letter of recommendation? Would they contract with an employment coach to ensure you can obtain employment at the same or higher level? If the answer is no or you are unsure, please take a moment to reflect on why prioritizing yourself and your needs feels greasy.

Not giving the work your all. Having an action plan does not mean that you don't give your current roles your best. If the work is truly your passion and what you were born to do, your employer is merely the platform for disseminating the work. You will always give the work your all and ensure you provide the human beings receiving your services with the highest quality of respect, care, and services possible.

Sometimes, we accept roles at widely known toxic organizations and organizations with high employee turnover rates. Entering these organizations without a goal and a great plan in place at the beginning sets you up for harm. It's comparable to looking at the forecast and seeing a 90% chance of rain and thunderstorms, then leaving your residence without your umbrella. The rain is not going to stop because you left your umbrella. The organization is not going to magically change because you arrived. They may have promised you that during your interview or even hired you to make those changes. The question is, where are the people who tried to make change before you? How are they doing? What has occurred within the organization to make the change more likely to happen now?

You are amazing, brilliant, and innovative, and still, with all of that, God did not give us the power to make people change. All we can do is plant seeds, model the way, and inspire change. People must first have the desire to want to change and then take consistent actions to manifest those changes. Believing anything different sets you up to be harmed, traumatized, and stuck. Be proactive and create your exit plan! Here are some example reflection questions.

- What are my personal, professional, and financial goals?

- What am I trying to achieve at this organization? What does success look like?

- If the organization is not what I thought it would be, and the clowns start falling off the shelf in ninety-one days, six months, or one year, how will I respond? What actions will I take?

- Who or what will support me in protecting my mind, body, and soul in the process?

Plan to Stay or Plan to Leave

You've got to learn to leave the table when love's no longer being served.

- Nina Simone

In my experience, the harm is greater when we enter the workplace based on the expectation that we will be respected, valued, celebrated, and treated equitably. There's absolutely nothing wrong with expecting that. However, we need more than expectations. What happens if your expectations and your experience don't align?

Based on my experiences, health, human, and social services organizations are some of the biggest contributors to Rough S.E.A.S. Employees join these organizations, eager to make a difference in the lives of individuals, families, and communities. They're excited to support them in thriving. Then, here comes the bull: the leader who is obsessed with power, politics, optics, and being in control. If you could just do your job with excellence and in peace, life at work would be amazing.

This is the place where many people get stuck, harmed, and severely injured, staying for the people while enduring significant harm in the process. We often do the opposite of what we educate our clients and customers to do. Would you encourage your client to stay in a toxic situation or relationship because they felt like they were making a difference?

We are so accustomed to being givers that we place ourselves at the mercy of others. What would you do if you were called into HR tomorrow and told the company no longer needed your services? What would your plan be? Creating an exit plan now is being proactive so you are not stuck. It gives you your power back so you can navigate with your eyes wide open, in strength and not fear. If you don't own your own company, at any point in time, you could be in a position that forces you to pivot. It could be by choice or force. This is the importance of developing a plan. Even if the organization you are working at is phenomenal, you should still have a plan. Think of it as your rainy-day account or insurance policy. If things start going sideways, you will be okay because you have proactively prepared an action plan.

I believe two plans are critical to reclaiming your power, wellness, and joy. Depending on your situation, you may implement one or both of them. I think it comes down to two options: either you are planning to leave, or you are planning to stay. Planning to stay means you foresee yourself at your current organization for one year or more. In this plan, you evaluate your goals and list the supports that help you protect and enhance your mind, body, and soul. Planning to leave means you foresee yourself at your current organization for less than one year. In this plan, you list the supports that will help you navigate difficult decisions and protect your mind, body, and soul in the process. You are also manifesting through action the things you desire and need while increasing your awareness of those things that are deal breakers and non-negotiable.

EITHER YOU ARE PLANNING TO LEAVE, OR YOU ARE PLANNING TO STAY.

Whatever you choose, you should decide that you will always have a plan. It should be a personal and living document. 'Personal' means it's specific to you, your situation, and your gifts. You decide who you would like to share it with. If you get stuck developing it, seek support from your tribe or trusted circle. The people close to you often know your strengths and the areas you excel in.

Soul Compass

What is your plan? Are you preparing to leave or preparing to stay?

Floaties

The goal of this section of the book is to advance to becoming a navigator. The "Floaties" subsection is designed to provide a summary of quick tips to develop the tools, mindset, and community necessary to become a navigator. The aim is to protect and reclaim your power, joy, and wellness. The goal is to become so confident that we no longer fight the waves but instead focus on enjoying the water and the surrounding Earth. We take out our floaties, surfboards, jet skis, and yachts.

- **Check your bag.**

    - The most important step to becoming a navigator is to believe in yourself. You have to believe that you can excel beyond your circumstances. Checking your bag requires you to inspect, remove, and rebrand any messaging that tells you that you are less than who you were created to be. Stand tall as your whole, beautiful, and brilliant Black self!

- **Self-care is a non-negotiable priority.**

    - There is only one YOU. Your health, well-being, joy, mind, body, and soul should precede everything. There are very few do-overs in life, so choose wisely what you put on hold and save for later. You are not promised time.

- **Grace and accountability should always be a compound action.**

    - Grace is unearned flexibility and forgiveness. When someone is accountable, they honor the grace given by taking responsibility for their actions and striving to make a positive difference.

- **Forgiveness is medicine for our soul.**

    - Forgive yourself and forgive others. Unforgiveness clogs our pipes of opportunities. Forgiveness frees up space for love, innovation, joy, good health, and many other positive things.

- **Change has receipts.**

    - Don't let anyone tell you change is on the way. Ask for receipts. Change should not be invisible. If there are no receipts, then there is likely no change on the way. Actions speak louder than words. Do not allow yourself to be abused and exploited, waiting on promised change.

- **Prepare for the rain.**

    - If it's raining on someone else's street or it's looking cloudy on your street, prepare for the rain. The clouds are a warning sign that something is on the horizon. Be proactive.

- **Always have a plan in place.**

    - Waiting until it rains to grab your umbrella is not a plan. Plan ahead and prepare to pivot. Plan to leave or plan to stay. This is key to protecting your physical, emotional, spiritual, and financial well-being.

CONSIDERATIONS

Tips for Black Women Leaders

- **Take healthy and positive actions to care for yourself.**

  - You are unique, and so is what you bring to the world. There will never be another you. Take care of yourself and prioritize your needs.

- **Use your vacation time before you feel burned out and overwhelmed.**

  - Find a healthy interval that enables you to engage in self-care versus after-care. Disconnect from work, even if you decide to just chill at home. Use your PTO time for mental and emotional rejuvenation to refill your well.

- **Therapy works.**

  - Finding a therapist specializing in working with individuals impacted by workplace culture toxicity can be invaluable. Some Black women therapists also specialize in working with Black women leaders.

- **You are the gift.**

  - Your gift lives within you. You were born with it. Your DNA, experiences, education, and life helped you to discover and refine it. Your job did not give you any gifts. God did. Never allow anyone to hold that over you. I don't care how much they've invested in you. They invested because they saw your potential, which was beneficial to them.

- **Find your people and community.**

  - Identify and engage in opportunities to be in a community with other leaders and healing-oriented spaces that can assist with refilling your well. Sunkissed Sunflower

Queens is a movement providing an accepting space that celebrates and uplifts Black women leaders (aspiring and experienced). Visit www.navigatingroughseas.com for more information.

- **Model healthy self-care practices for your team members and colleagues.**

  - This will reduce your need to be their buffer and protector. It also helps with developing boundaries. Cultivate their skills and support them in advocating for themselves. These life skills are sustainable over the long term.

- **Remember people and their behaviors.**

  - You will see them again in a different workplace, with a different name, gender, race/ethnicity, etc. The more you learn how to navigate personalities, the better you will navigate the workplace and life.

- **Stop recommending people to work in toxic environments.**

  - If this is not an option, try to avoid painting the office culture as phenomenal and thriving if it's not. There are professional ways to share the organization's areas for growth and improvement. This enables individuals to adjust their expectations and activate the skills necessary to navigate the organization's culture and leadership.

- **Leave the toxic situation.**

  - Sometimes, this means finding a better position or making a lateral move. Sometimes, it may mean taking a step back to recuperate so you can move forward.

- **Pouring into YOU. The rule of 200%.**

    Whatever you give your work, give yourself double, at minimum. If you give your job 100%, give yourself 200%. Make regular deposits into your well-being and life. This can look like taking a break for your favorite ice cream, scheduling time for exercise or meditation, watching a video that makes you laugh, being in a community with others, going on a vacation or staycation, getting a massage, or engaging in other things that make your heart smile. Taking time just to breathe and be is a powerful form of self-care.

Tips for Career Seekers

Before You Say Yes

Research the organization before you say yes. Every organization has a culture. A culture exists in the employee handbook and on the organization's website. Then, there is the organizational culture that is unwritten, which is the most powerful. These are the real rules of engagement and how the organization ascribes to and reinforces them through penalties and promotions. It's the culture that you just so happen to stumble upon or be gut-punched with after you are employed and have passed your probationary period. If it takes that long.

Review the organization's website and social media platforms. You can learn a lot about an organization based on its digital footprint, or lack thereof. In my experience, you can often go to an organization's website and learn a lot about its culture through the language used, photos used, programs and services, and the demographics of its staff, board, and leadership team. You can also learn about their mission, vision, and values. If they post board minutes, you can learn the priorities of the organization and the board's level of commitment and participation. If they post their employee handbook, you can learn more about the written guidelines the organization holds its employees to.

To learn about the organization's unwritten rules, you need to know someone who works or worked there, read the public reviews from former employees, or ask relevant questions during your interview. If they post client or customer survey results, you can also learn from those. Be mindful of the number of respondents and their demographics. You can learn a lot about an organization's priorities on other social media sites through their posts, pictures, and comments. Here are a few questions to consider as you navigate the career prospecting process.

- What is the organization's story?

- What are their stated mission, vision, and values?

- What receipts do they have?

- What are the demographics of the organization's staff? Leadership team? Board? Community partners? Clients?

- Who funds the organization? What is the history of their funders?

- What are their goals for hiring you? Have they ever hired someone like you? How did that work out? Is this person(s) still there?

- What politics does the organization navigate?

- What are your goals? What are the organization's goals? Is there alignment?

Lastly, an interview should be a two-way conversation. The organization's interviewers should not be the only people asking questions. As a prospective employee, you should actively participate in asking questions and determining if the organization is a good fit for your values, goals, and lifestyle. I have often seen people come to interviews so excited about the possibility of being hired that they position themselves as docile interviewees. I have been guilty of this throughout my career until I learned better and understood my value and power as an asset to the prospective employer. We spend numerous hours at work, so the least we can do is ask questions to better understand how we will spend our time at the organization. It's the equivalent of going to a car dealership and allowing the salesperson to sell you a vehicle without test driving it, inquiring about the warranty, payments, or other specifics related to the make and model. This would not be the wisest process, and there is a great chance that we would endure unnecessary stress, potential exploitation, and harm due to neglecting due diligence. We wouldn't do this with a vehicle; our lives are significantly more valuable than any vehicle. So, we should value our time, lives, peace, wellness, and joy enough to protect them.

> AS A PROSPECTIVE EMPLOYEE, YOU SHOULD ACTIVELY PARTICIPATE IN ASKING QUESTIONS AND DETERMINING IF THE ORGANIZATION IS A GOOD FIT FOR YOUR VALUES, GOALS, AND LIFESTYLE.

After You Say Yes

While leaving the grocery store one day, I passed by two employees on break. One employee was talking about a workplace experience when the other employee responded, "There's going to be some shit anywhere you go." I agreed and laughed. She was absolutely correct. There will always be something to navigate in the workplace because we work with imperfect and unhealed humans. Does it make it right? No. Should we expect it? In my opinion, absolutely. What would it look like if you were proactive and diligent about finding the shit? Finding the shit before the shit finds you and punches you in the gut when you least expect it.

Hopefully, if you present as trustworthy and sincere, someone who cares may take a risk to pull you aside and share what you can expect or at least validate your experiences. Otherwise, it becomes a game of mental Minesweeper, walking lightly and praying that you don't mess around and find out. Some employers have labeled this as gossiping. Labeling is a tactic for shutting down undesirable conversations between team members. Is there such a thing as office gossiping? There absolutely is. However, I don't deem it as gossip if it is a factual conversation with the goal of supporting a team in navigating a toxic workplace more "safely." It's harm reduction. You deserve to belong, you deserve to be psychologically safe at work, and you deserve to be in a community with others who can offer support and strategies.

> YOU DESERVE TO BELONG, YOU DESERVE TO BE PSYCHOLOGICALLY SAFE AT WORK, AND YOU DESERVE TO BE IN A COMMUNITY WITH OTHERS WHO CAN OFFER SUPPORT AND STRATEGIES.

Power

Stop, watch, look, and listen. Where does the primary power lie? Is it shared or concentrated? How is power used? To uplift, inspire, celebrate, or empower individuals, or to oppress, censor, manipulate, and abuse individuals? There are many types of power. However, I will highlight two: the power of influence and the power of decision-making.

The power of decision-making. Certain individuals have the authority and the power to make decisions within the organization. It's often found in a hierarchical document, such as an organizational chart. This is necessary for balance and structure within the organization. Could you imagine if everyone in the organization could initiate and submit grants or have access to the organization's banking and investment accounts? Without a process and strategy, it would be a hot mess, and the organization would most likely be out of business within a short period of time.

The power of influence. Sometimes, we assume power lies solely in the C-suites and board. Sometimes it does, and sometimes it does not. While the power of decision-making ultimately lies in these sections of the organization, the power to influence decisions may lie within other sections of the organization. I have worked in organizations where the power of influence was the food pantry manager, executive assistant, human resources, direct services staff, or a leader at an external community organization. These individuals did not possess the authority to make decisions. Still, they heavily influenced the decision, and sometimes it was their decision and sometimes their written rationale or statement that appeared with the signature of a C-suite authority.

Environment

Be mindful of your environment. I like to think of the workplace environment in terms of a game. My goal is to identify the games being played. Candyland (children's games), Big Brother (groups and clubs), Operation (penalties and censorship), Monopoly (all about the money), Scrabble (word games), and other games. Knowing the games being played, your role, and what you can do to survive and maybe succeed is essential. Knowing prevents you from showing up to play football in your basketball uniform. You would be seriously hurt. People get hurt when they don't know a game is being played, are in denial, or don't prepare effectively. Choosing how you show up and adjusting your expectations allows you to be proactive. Otherwise, you may be caught off guard and forced to be reactive. The goal is to reduce workplace trauma through awareness, preparation, and responsiveness.

Exploitation Versus Experience

It is important to know the difference between exploitation and experience. Some leaders are genuinely interested in supporting you in building your knowledge, skills, abilities, and network as long as there is alignment with the organization. Some leaders are genuinely interested in supporting you in thriving as an employee and human being, even if your dreams will take you beyond the organization or their department. As a leader, I strive for the latter option. I have been blessed throughout my career to have a few leaders who saw me and were not overly threatened by my goals. They nurtured me as much as their role and capacity allowed. This made a significant impact on my life. It doesn't take much. One leader can pour into you and make a positive difference that ripples throughout your entire career. This is the leader that I strive to be and the leadership legacy that I desire to cultivate. If I can be that one, you can be that one, and we can be the ones to make the workplace better.

On the opposite end of the spectrum, some leaders intentionally select new graduates and individuals new to the industry/role, those with little to moderate experience, and those with low confidence and self-esteem. Their goal is to manipulate the mindsets of these individuals. You would be surprised by the impact of a first "real" check and its benefits in influencing and manipulating someone's thought processes. What would you do for a "real" paycheck? I have seen employees side with and even defend leaders causing harm. I have seen team members devalue the actions of advocates by labeling them as disingenuous, performative, or fake. I have seen team members bully other team members for standing up against racism, microaggressions, gaslighting, and other forms of oppression. What would you do for a real paycheck? Hopefully, not any of these things. The person who oppresses others is the same person who oppresses you. Open your eyes, ask curious questions, avoid placing icing on a rotten cake, and dig to the roots of the intentions and actions of those around you. Paychecks should be payments for work performed, not tokens of manipulation. This is why it's essential to know yourself and have some sense of direction for who you are striving to be, where you are striving to go, and your why. Otherwise, you leave yourself vulnerable to rip currents that lead to manipulation and harm.

As a new employee, there are several things that you need to be aware of. This book contains many. However, there are still many that have not been discussed. Here is a list of reflection questions that may support you in examining situations that arise in your workplace.

- Identify the topic, situation, occurrence, or trend.

- Who is it benefiting? In what ways?

- Who is being harmed, censored, or negatively impacted? In what ways?

- Where are there opportunities for reconciliation, improvement, and growth? What is the organization's stance, and what are its actions regarding these opportunities?

- What power or influence do you possess in this situation?

- What plan of action can you implement?

Tips for Allies in Leadership

Allies get wet. - Mordecai Dixon

"Ally" is a noun and a verb. An ally is, and an ally does. Allies take uncomfortable risks. They get wet because they get in the water with the people they support and advocate on behalf of, not in the shallow but deep waters. Anyone can stand in the sand or shallow water when things get tough, unpopular, or when retaliation occurs from those who refuse to change. Being in deep water means you get wet. It means your stance is visible to others and demonstrates your commitment to the movement of equity and justice. Allyship is not only standing up in support of something that contributes to the well-being, safety, and health of a person or group. It's also taking a stance against harmful things, even when you or someone you love is benefiting from the same circumstances. Here are a few reflection questions to consider.

AN ALLY IS, AND AN ALLY DOES.

- What actions are you willing to take? Are you willing to stand tall and strong, or is your approach quiet or passive?

- When are you willing to do it? When it's convenient and comfortable, or when it's uncomfortable and scary?

- Who are you willing to stand up to? Are you willing to stand up to funders, friends, board members, customers/clients, business partners, colleagues, and co-workers in positions of power?

- Are you willing to risk losing a relationship, money, or favor?

If you answered no, maybe, or erred on the side of quiet and passive to any of the questions above, then I strongly encourage you to self-reflect and reevaluate the status of your allyship. How are your stance and actions impacting historically marginalized staff and colleagues? Positively or negatively? There is no such thing as a neutral impact. You're either helping or harming. As Black women, we don't need silent, savior, fair-weather, or faux allies. We need people who are first willing to do their work and then commit to standing up and using their power, voices, roles, and privileges to take actions that consistently improve the experiences of Black women and other marginalized identities in the workplace. If you are or seriously aspire to be an ally for Black women in the workplace, thank you for your support. Here are a few tips for consideration.

- **Listen and believe Black women when they share their workplace experiences.**

    - Avoid gaslighting and racelighting. Ensure that your questions come from a place of curious learning. It should not feel like an interrogation or cross-examination. It's painful enough to determine if we should speak up, what we should say, and who we should say it to. It takes a lot of courage to speak up and replay a harmful experience. Just because you have not experienced the person in this manner does not mean the experience is untrue or we are being too sensitive.

- **Take action swiftly.**

    - Mean what you say, and follow up with quick action. Make time to address the harm being done in the organization. If there were a large funding opportunity that required a quick turnaround, an urgent request from your current funder, or a demand from the IRS, you would drop everything, prioritize it, and make time to respond. Addressing workplace harms should garner the same level of attention and intensity of response.

- **Follow through.**

  - Band-aid responses exacerbate the harm. Don't facilitate a one-time response and never follow up. There should be ongoing conversations, continuous follow-ups, and check-ins with those who were most impacted, as well as those who contributed to the harm, to assess the status of the situation on an ongoing basis.

- **Continue to do your self-work.**

  - Too often, the weight of education is placed on those harmed. As a leader, you can serve as a lid or a bridge. As a lid, the growth of team members is limited by your growth, fragility, fears, experiences, biases, self-reflection, and more. As a bridge, you help others grow as you grow and connect them with resources that extend beyond your capacity. Your index finger is a mighty creation! It can click a mouse for an internet search, turn a page in a book, or phone a buddy for a conversation.

- **Engage in daily self-reflection and self-work.**

  - Engaging in intentional self-work is necessary for an effective and equitable leader. There are no substitutes or workarounds. One workshop, one conversation, one Black friend, one book, and one podcast or documentary will never be sufficient. Active learning is needed every day!

- **Engage in lifelong learning.**

  - There will never be a point where any of us have arrived. Learning, unlearning, and relearning is a challenging and lifelong process. If you grew up in a household where racism or self-hate was normalized, cultivated, and perpetuated, that lives in you. If it's not acknowledged and checked daily, it will become a reflexive way of being, thinking, believing, acting, and making decisions.

Reflect on how you show up.

Think about how you use your position and power. How do you intend to use it? What impact would you like to make? What impact are you actually making? How are Black women experiencing you and your leadership?

We don't need another hero.

Black women don't need to be rescued or saved or told how to behave. We have navigated the world and workplace long enough to write a series of books and movies.

Find an accountability buddy.

An accountability buddy is a person(s) who will hold you accountable for being an effective ally. Someone who you can ask curious and uncomfortable questions. Someone who tells you to stop and sit down when you are doing harm. They need to be able to do this without fearing that you will retaliate or shut down. Remember, this is someone who cares and wants to see you be the best leader and human possible.

Get help.

If you are contributing to harm and genuinely care, seek appropriate help and follow through. You deserve to get better! Your team and colleagues deserve to know the best version of YOU, the person you were created to be. Find a therapist, coach, or other support to help you.

- **Develop a plan of action.**

  - Use the information you already know to take action. I have seen many organizational leaders survey staff and do nothing. What do you already know because it has already been shared? What is one action step that you can take with that information today?

- **Support Black women in finding their communities.**

  - Black women need support that extends beyond your organization. Support Black women by supporting opportunities for them to be in communities with other Black and Brown people. This includes but is not limited to paying for professional support subscriptions or training events. Adjust how you view Black women when they come together during their breaks or decide to go to lunch together. If you are not invited to join, don't take it upon yourself to tag along, guilt trip the group for not inviting you, or "remind" them that they need to return by a certain time to assert control.

RESOURCES

Navigating toxic and harmful work environments is serious. It can be extremely traumatic and result in physical, mental health, and emotional challenges and manifestations. Research demonstrates a connection between workplace abuse or mistreatment and suicidal ideations and attempts. This should not be taken lightly—urgent attention and care are critical. It's important that you seek help and support immediately if you are navigating a challenging work environment. Whether the work environment is in person, virtual/online, or hybrid does not matter. Workplace harm can be experienced regardless of the setting, industry, field, role, or reputation of the organization. If you are being harmed, you are not being petty, too sensitive, too soft, or too dramatic; you are being a human. Listening to your mind and body is critical to your wellness. Seek help and support. You matter. Your life matters. Your well-being matters. Please prioritize YOU. Listed below is a short list of resources.

988 Suicide & Crisis Lifeline

24/7, free and confidential support for people in distress, prevention and crisis resources for you or your loved ones, and best practices for professionals in the U.S.

Website: https://988lifeline.org/

Phone Number: 988

National Alliance on Mental Illness (NAMI)

Provides education, support, and advocacy to individuals and family members who are navigating mental illness. Maintains a national database of local programs throughout the U.S.

Website: https://www.nami.org/

Psychology Today

A virtual directory of therapists, psychologists, and other mental health professionals. A cool thing about the directory is that you can sort by location, insurance type, specialty, gender, faith, and more. You can also view photos, bios, and introduction videos of selected practitioners to get a feel for them, their personalities, and their style.

Website: https://www.psychologytoday.com/us

Soul Care for Black Clinicians, LaTanya Tolan

A licensed clinical social worker (LCSW) who provides life coaching and mental health therapy to Black clinicians and healers.

Website: https://soulcareforblackclinicians.com/

The AntiHR, HR Lady, S. Anne Marie Archer

HR consultancy specializing in getting out of discriminatory and hostile work environments.

Website: https://www.theantihr-hrlady.com/

YouTube Channel: https://www.youtube.com/channel/UC-58Ilf3YUU9NyqHTqpSYfg

ABOUT THE AUTHOR

Be Bold! Be Brave! Be You!

I am an equity and justice tigress! I have always been uniquely agitated by inequities, injustices, and unnecessary suffering. There has always been a fire within me to advocate loudly, support unique needs, and exceed the expectations of historically marginalized individuals and groups.

As a young girl in elementary school, I had aspirations of becoming a pediatric nurse practitioner and a civil rights attorney. I had it all figured out, too. I would work as a lawyer during the day and as a nurse practitioner in the evenings. As I got older, I realized the schedule would be exhausting and unsustainable. As a teenager, I was fortunate to attend a high school that offered vocational academies. This enabled me to pursue nursing as a high school student, engage in clinicals at the local hospital and nursing home, and take my state exams to become a Certified Nursing Assistant. During my high school clinical experiences, I observed inequities in patient care and facility amenities. These inequities were created by differences in insurance types and socioeconomic status, which ultimately intersected with race and created a hierarchy of quality of care and quality of life. There was the regular and short staff side of this nursing home, and then there was the wealthy side of the nursing home. Based on the artifacts and smell, you would know which side you were on. This was very unsettling.

In college, I started out in nursing and later switched my major to Health Education. Educating individuals from marginalized groups and communities in a way that was engaging and easy to understand was and remains something that excites me, challenges me, and makes my heart smile.

I believe everyone should have opportunities and access to culturally responsive and engaging information that supports them in being the best and healthiest version of themselves. I quickly learned the best way to see change is to create it myself, either by being at decision-making tables or creating my own. This led me to pursue my master's and doctorate degrees in management and leadership concentrations. My goal extends beyond providing a service; my goal is to cultivate experiences, whether it be with clients, patients, providers, or community members. I want people to remember their experiences with me because they feel uniquely seen, heard, believed, and valued.

Although I am not working as a lawyer during the day and a pediatric nurse practitioner in the evenings, that yearning to serve in the realm of health and law has stayed with me. I believe it's true that we are born with our purpose and that we refine it through our life experiences. I am thankful that my education and career have brought me to the intersection of fulfilling my purpose of nursing and law in so many other ways on a daily basis. This has opened many doors and opportunities for me to follow in the light of others and develop my own path. I believe my work is to educate, mentor, train, and support others in cultivating positive experiences for those they serve. As the saying goes, charity begins at home; I believe home training begins with leaders and their beliefs and mindset. Then it moves to their first customer, which is their staff. Then to their clients, customers, colleagues, and community members.

More About Me

Dr. Tonicia Freeman-Foster is a national consultant, trainer, and coach with over 20 years of experience in leading and guiding equitable and culturally responsive programming that uplifts historically underserved individuals and marginalized communities. Dr. Freeman-Foster serves as the CEO and Co-Founder of LEIDOSWEL™.

Dr. Freeman-Foster has held formal leadership positions for a significant portion of her career. She has navigated and is a navigator of Rough S.E.A.S. She is extremely passionate about organizational culture and leaders' power to make their workplaces, communities, systems, services, and the world a better place for all people. She is equally passionate about leadership accountability and supporting leaders in building their personal and professional capacity to lead healthy workplaces that stand against racism, inequities, injustices, and oppression of all forms. Dr. Freeman-Foster's dream is diverse, inclusive, progressive, innovative, and human-centered workplaces where employees and clients achieve their fullest potential.

Dr. Freeman-Foster possesses a bachelor's degree in community health, a master's degree in organizational management and leadership, and a doctorate degree in organizational leadership. She is certified as a healing circle practitioner, coach, diversity professional, health education specialist, and project management professional.

To learn more about Dr. Freeman-Foster's credentials, publications, and work, please connect with her on LinkedIn: www.linkedin.com/in/toniciaff

ABOUT LEIDOSWEL™

LEIDOSWEL™ is a company that provides consulting and coaching experiences that transform leaders and organizations one action at a time.

Our mission is to inspire and support leaders to be the change they wish to see in the world through self-reflection and positive actions. We teach leaders how to make meaningful differences in their lives, workplaces, and communities through innovative strategies and intentional everyday actions by focusing on three leadership pillars: Learn Well, Lead Well, and Live Well. Our vision is bold leaders equipped with the resources and confidence to take action and foster positive individual, organizational, community, and systems-level transformations.

We offer unique leadership consulting, training, coaching, mentoring, and community learning experiences to our clients. A sample of our offerings is listed below.

Navigating Rough S.E.A.S.

- The Seven Waves of Rough S.E.A.S. Navigation Tool ™

    Is your organization on a mission to cultivate a workplace experience where employees love to come and hate to leave? To achieve this goal, you must understand the current climate and culture of your organization. Once this is identified, a plan can be developed to support your staff and foster organizational success. This learning experience assists organizations in understanding how their staff perceive and interact in the organization. With this, organizations can develop strategies to improve the employee experience through action planning and individual and group coaching.

- Sunkissed Sunflower Queens

    Are you a Black woman in a leadership role and seeking a supportive community to be a part of? Sunkissed Sunflower Queens is a supportive professional development community for Black women in leadership.

To learn more about these opportunities, please visit: www.navigatingroughseas.com

Professional Development Learning Experiences

- Cultivating Organizations That WOW!

    Supports organizational leaders in developing their leadership legacy. Participants also assess their organization and develop a plan that supports employees, clients/customers, and community members in reaching their full potential.

- An Ally C.A.A.R.E.S

    An Ally Care-Accountability-Action-Reconciliation-Equity-Self-Reflection is a compassionate and non-judgmental community learning experience for allies who want to do more and improve how they show up in their workplaces and communities.

To learn more about these learning experiences, please visit www.leidoswel.com.

ACKNOWLEDGEMENTS

Writing this book has been a journey filled with so many emotions. I am still pinching myself in disbelief that I opened my vault of notes and ideas I have written over several years and am actually publishing this book. Life is best done in a community with people who support, push, and inspire you.

First and foremost, I want to thank God for life, health, strength, grace, and mercy. Without Him, there would be no me. I am grateful for the life that He has given me. It has been a journey, and I have learned so much about myself along the way. The valleys do not define me; they refine me and help me to clarify my mission and purpose. Thank you, God, for joy, illuminating my path, bestowing within me the tools and expertise to navigate my journey, and the opportunity to celebrate life with amazing human beings. I am committed to lifelong learning, growing, and evolving. Breath=Life=Opportunity.

My next huge thank you is to my best friend and husband, Terrell. Thank you for your presence. Thank you for being my rock and an unwavering, consistent, and loving force in my life. Thank you for holding things down, which allowed me the time and space to complete this book. Thank you for participating in my spur-of-the-moment idea, grammar, review, and jam sessions. Thank you for your unconditional love, inspiration, prayers, support, encouragement, compassion, listening ear, shoulder to cry on, celebration respites, and laughs. Thank you for believing in me. I love you!

Thank you to my parents for giving me life, inspiring me, and pouring into me even as an adult. God has a way of showing you how much you are loved. I am grateful for my two moms, Gloria (my birth mom) and Gillian (my Earth mom), and my dad, Leon. Thank you for your unconditional love, support, prayers, belief in my dreams, the laughs, the questions, feedback, and presence in my life. Thank you for being my parents and my friends. To my Earth mom, Gillian, and dad, Leon, I extend additional gratitude for taking the time to listen to every podcast or radio show I participate in, reading every article I publish, reviewing photos, book covers, etc., and providing real feedback, even when the shows and articles were lengthy. I'm still working on that! Thank you to my family members. I appreciate each of you, your love, support, and encouragement. Grandma Mae, you hold a very special place in my heart. Just hearing your voice and laugh brightens my day! Thank you to my elders and ancestors. I love you all!

Every captainess needs a crew and shipmates for a successful voyage. Days at sea are fun, but my favorite is the ports of call. The opportunities to explore, engage with others, bask in the surrounding beauty, and celebrate. These supportive, refueling, and replenishment stations are not just fun but critical to the journey. Thank you to the individuals who have poured into me and have helped me be a better person. Here are some of my ports of call. If I've missed anyone, please charge it to my head, not my heart.

Brotha Mordecai Dixon, you are an amazing and brilliant human being! The world needs to know you. Our jam sessions are always full of great wisdom and strategies. I think we have created positive world change a few times. Thank you for dreaming with me. Thank you to your beautiful wife and family for allowing me the opportunity to take up your time.

Alicja Carter, my sista from another mista. Thank you for being my friend, ally, and great supporter. Your curiosity and thoughtful inquiries inspire and stretch me. You are an amazing human being with so many gifts and talents, and you always seek to selflessly share them with the world. Thank you for inspiring me. Thank you for being you.

Kathy Taylor and LaTanya Tolan (soon to be Dr. Tolan), my sistas and fire twins, thank you for your time, support, love, feedback, powerful live prayers, ideas, laughs, and our jam sessions. Thank you for challenging me, believing in me, holding me accountable, and encouraging me to believe in myself. Thank you for being amazing human beings, period. I am so blessed that God allowed our paths to cross and intersect in so many ways.

Godmother Margaret Dawson-Brown, Sonya Foster, Shirlisa Mapp, Carl Lavender, Jr., Dr. Barbara Morrison-Rodriguez, Ashley Singleton, Ja'net Higgins-Weston, Kha McTier, Cassie Montes, Tajhah Kittling, Evelyn Clark, Jennifer Ratliff, Dr. Adrienne George, Dr. Carmen Reese Foster, Queens Bee & Zee and the Zumba Queens, Dr. Julie Radlauer-Doerfler, Molly Kennedy, and Scott VanLoo. Thank you to each of you for your kind words, gestures, support, encouragement, thoughtfulness, laughs, belief in me, and cheers over the years. Thank you for your vision of seeing me as an author before I saw it myself.

I am blessed to have the most phenomenal coaches and gift development team! A huge shout-out and gratitude to Attorney Coach Jamila Moore, Dr. Avis Jones-DeWeever, Coach Jalima Cook, Coach Anita Watkins, Coach Tye Miles, and Yolanda Churchwell. Thank you for your time, energy, expertise, and wisdom. Thank you for believing in me, challenging me, and selflessly pouring into me.

To my book and publishing coach, Reea Rodney, at Dara Publishing and her amazing team. Thank you for being a boss! Thank you for inspiring me with your innovative ideas, believing in me, and holding me extra accountable to being progressive and completing this book.

Last but certainly of great importance, thank you to all of the Black women who encouraged and inspired me through your excitement to tell my story, which belongs to all of us, birthing this book. Please continue to keep your heads up. You are seen, loved, heard, and valued. Create a plan to protect your power, wellness, joy, and peace. Love and prioritize yourself.

Much love, admiration, and gratitude, queens. I salute each of you!

We are our ancestors' wildest dreams!

ENDNOTES

Agbanobi, A. & Asmelash, T. V. (2023). Creating Psychological Safety for Black Women at Your Company. Harvard Business Review. https://hbr.org/2023/05/creating-psychological-safety-for-black-women-at-your-company

American Psychological Association. APA poll reveals toxic workplaces, other significant workplace mental health challenges. (2023, July 13). https://www.apa.org. https://www.apa.org/news/press/releases/2023/07/work-mental-health-challenges

Bell, C.C. (1980). Racism: a symptom of the narcissistic personality disorder. *Journal of the National Medical Association, 72*(7), 661–665.

Corbett, H. (2022, February 22). How to be an ally for Black women in the workplace. Forbes. https://www.forbes.com/sites/hollycorbett/2022/02/22/how-to-be-an-ally-for-black-women-in-the-workplace/?sh=357016453123

Dignity Together (2023). Study shows prolonged exposure to workplace abuse can lead to suicide – and it can happen to anyone. https://www.dignitytogether.org/blog/study-shows-prolonged-exposure-to-workplace-bullying-can-lead-to-suicide-and-it-can-happen-to-anyone

Every Level Leadership. (2022, August 2). Black Women Thriving Report - Every level leadership. https://everylevelleads.com/bwt

FreshBooks. (2023, April 18). How many hours does the average person work per week? https://www.freshbooks.com/hub/productivity/how-many-hours-does-the-average-person-work

Gladwell, M. *(2002). The tipping point: How little things can make a big difference. Back Bay Books.*

Gupta, S. (2022, August 15). What is the narcissistic abuse cycle? Verywell Mind. https://www.verywellmind.com/narcissistic-abuse-cycle-stages-impact-and-coping-6363187#toc-stages-of-the-narcissistic-abuse-cycle

Lean In. (2021). Key findings from Women in the Workplace 2021. https://leanin.org/women-in-the-workplace-2021

Lloyd, B. C. (2023, July 21). Black women in the workplace. Gallup.com. https://www.gallup.com/workplace/333194/black-women-workplace.aspx

Magnusson Hanson, L. L., Pentti, J., Nordentoft, M., Xu, T., Rugulies, R., Madsen, I. E. H., Conway, P. M., Westerlund, H., Vahtera, J., Ervasti, J., Batty, G. D., & Kivimäki, M. (2023). Association of workplace violence and bullying with later suicide risk: a multicohort study and meta-analysis of published data. The Lancet. Public health, 8(7), e494–e503. https://doi.org/10.1016/S2468-2667(23)00096-8

Mind Share Partners. (2023). Mind Share Partners' 2023 Mental Health At Work Report. https://www.mindsharepartners.org/mentalhealthatworkreport-2023

Office of the Surgeon General. (2022). Workplace Mental Health & Well-Being — current priorities of the U.S. Surgeon General. U.S. Department of Health & Human Services. https://www.hhs.gov/surgeongeneral/priorities/workplace-well-being/index.html

Reese, M. (2022, August 25). A point of view: soar when you soar in response to 'Pet to threat.' The Inclusion Solution. https://theinclusionsolution.me/a-point-of-view-soar-when-you-soar-in-response-to-pet-to-threat/

Tipping point. *(2023). In Merriam-Webster Dictionary. https://www.merriam-webster.com/dictionary/tipping%20point*

Thank You

Dear Treasured Readers,

Thank you from the depths of my heart for choosing to embark on this journey with my book. Your time and engagement mean the world to me. If you found the book insightful or empowering, I would be immensely grateful if you could take a moment to share your thoughts by leaving a review on Amazon. Your feedback is invaluable and helps others discover the book.

Warmest regards,

Dr. Tonicia Freeman-Foster

www.ingramcontent.com/pod-product-compliance
Lightning Source LLC
Chambersburg PA
CBHW050519100526
44581CB00001B/31